£3.00

D0119971

OWLS

OWLS

•CHRIS MEAD•

with illustrations by
GUY TROUGHTON

Whittet Books

(Endpaper illustration) Little Owl
(Half-title illustration) Long-eared Owl
(Title illustration) Barn Owl

First published 1987
Text © 1987 by Chris Mead
Illustrations © 1987 by Guy Troughton
Whittet Books Ltd, 18 Anley Road, London W14 0BY

Design by Richard Kelly

British Library Cataloguing in Publication Data

Mead, Chris
    Owls. —— (Natural history).
    1. Owls —— Great Britain
    2. Birds —— Great Britain
    I. Title II. Series
    598'.97'0941   QL696.S8
ISBN 0–905483–59–6

Typeset by Systemset Composition, London NW2
Printed and bound by Oxford University Press Printing House

Contents

Introduction 7

What is an owl? 8

Evolving owls 14

British owls 15

Euro-owls 24

Sound pictures 32

Owl talk 36

Seeing in the dark 37

Feet are for killing 43

Pellets 45

The owl's menu 50

Display 55

The nest 56

Nest-boxes 61

Sex and the single owl 68

Breeding seasons 70

Owl eggs 71

Just a'sittin' and a'waitin' 73

How many eggs to lay? 75

Growing up 77

Owls on the move 80

Nomads 84

Town owl, country owl 85

Roosting 86

Territoriality 88

Internecine strife 89

How many owls? 91

Owl count 94

Beware 97

Mobbing 99

Toxic chemicals 101

Longevity 102

Parasites and disease 103

Accidents 104

First aid 107

Breeding for release 110

Owls and gamekeepers 112

Protective acts 113

Folklore 116

Scientific names explained 118

Country names 120

Wise old owl 122

Studying owls 124

Further reading 126

Index 128

Introduction

'O' is for owl. So familiar an image that it is one of the classics of the children's alphabet; most often the owl depicted will be a Tawny or Barn. There are in fact more than 130 species of owls worldwide and 5 well distributed in Britain.

This book concentrates on the British species, with some reference to a further 10 European ones and a few of the more exotic owls from further afield – what book about owls could pass over the amazing owls that have taken to fishing for a living? They are carnivorous birds which are, for the most part, nocturnal equivalents of the hawks and falcons of the day. They have large eyes and most have very well developed ears giving them a big-headed appearance. They perch upright and look exactly like our idea of an owl.

This big-headed appearance with the upright stance is probably one of the main reasons why owls are so beloved by humans. Most birds and animals that are considered to be particularly 'cuddly' have human characteristics, and some of the worst excesses of selective breeding – of animals as diverse as pigeons and dogs – have sought to flatten the animal's face and provide more 'human' features – though sometimes the process works in reverse, too, with the humans looking more like their dogs.

The real lives of the owls, the ways that they have become physically adapted for their life-style and the many behavioural tricks they regularly employ are just as fascinating as the stories told about their mysterious ways culled from folk memory. The eerie presence of screeching, hooting and snoring creatures round the local ruins at night would have been expected to give them a rather bad press. Luckily for them, and happily for us, the image of the wise old owl is the lasting one.

Tawny Owl.

What is an owl?

Dictionaries tell us that owls are nocturnal rapacious birds with big heads, flat faces and an upright stance. That is a good start, but, as always, even the most obvious generalities are not always true. For instance by no means all the species of owls living today are wholly nocturnal. Their special adaptations show that the ancestors of the owls were all night birds many millions of years ago. As life evolved and the day time became dangerous for small furry things, many of them took to a nocturnal existence to escape predators. The ancestral owls were on to a 'good thing' in exploiting their prey when they had to come out into the open to lead their lives – that is, at night. Nowadays species like the Short-eared Owl are very well adapted to a day-time life-style and are a familiar sight 'quartering' (ranging up and down) the open ground of moorland or new forestry plantations at all hours of the day.

Superficially owls seem to be close relatives of the diurnal (daytime) birds of prey – hawks, falcons, eagles and harriers. They share a strongly hooked beak adapted for tearing at the flesh of their prey and sharp-toed, grasping feet for striking at and holding their victims. However, as with many other characteristics found throughout the natural world, the explanation for this close similarity is 'convergent evolution' (nature finding the same solution to a problem by two different routes). Owls are not really at all closely related to birds of prey but because their habits are so very similar the equipment that they have evolved has inevitably become very much the same.

Most owls are overall brown or grey in colour with a very soft, loose plumage and surprisingly small bodies within the extravagant covering of feathers. The soft feathers serve both to keep their movements quiet and also to insulate them during the coldness of the night – particularly important since so many species perch, immobile, on a vantage point for long periods waiting for prey to become available. They have very well developed sight and hearing with extra-large eyes and very special ear openings. In several species the ears are asymmetrical, which means the birds can hear different frequencies better with one ear than the other. For a few species even their skulls are asymmetrical but with most it is just the external fleshy ear openings that are different. The reason for this seemingly pointless adaptation is given on p.33. Incidentally the ear tufts worn by a number of species are nothing to do with hearing but have a part to play in species recognition and, possibly, camouflage by breaking up the smooth, rounded outline of the head.

Owls are big-headed simply because they have so much to fit in – and point forward – on their faces. They have very large eyes – the biggest species have bigger eyes than humans do – also very well developed ears and wide facial discs. This disc is present on all owl species but particularly well developed in some, like the Barn Owl. It consists of many rings of stiff feathers surrounding the bird's eyes – in the case of the Barn Owl forming a rounded, heart-shaped pattern – and with a definite border of slightly bigger, stiff feathers at its edge. The facial disc is thought to be very important in helping the bird to focus its hearing on particular sounds. This may be by using the same principle as the parabolic reflector used for sound or the focusing mirror on a torch. Alternatively it may be that the disc's main function is to allow the sounds to reach the bird's ears without being drowned by wind noise: the owl's microphone muff!

Most owls nest in holes and all have rather round chalky white eggs. The total lack of any markings to the eggs is probably a very good indication that the owls, and their ancestors, have been hole-nesting birds for millions of years. Birds that nest in the open usually evolve pigmented eggs, often with elaborate patterns, which may be to aid parental recognition or to help conceal the eggs from predators, if they are left unattended. As we shall see, many species of owls are able to regulate their clutch size to match the available food supply.

Another characteristic of owls is their ability, indeed need, to bring up pellets of indigestible food. These vary in size, shape and even colour according to the species. The remains of the birds, insects, fish, frogs and, above all, small mammals which the bird has caught and eaten are readily indentifiable in the pellets – after they have been collected and teased apart. This means we have been able to study the diet of owls in great detail. It has also proved very useful for scientists working on small mammals who have often been able to map the distribution of shy, nocturnal species by looking at owl pellets rather than going to the trouble of setting their own trap-lines.

Of course, being nocturnal, owls cannot see each other when they are most active and so they communicate a great deal by sound. The calls can seem to vary a great deal but the characteristic sounds of the different species of owl are generally very easy to tell apart. The calls used for territorial advertisement are often rather simple with a standard rhythm for each species, although often the pitch of the calls will vary within a broad range. The calls are certainly loud – the bigger species are often audible, on a quiet night without too much wind, over distances of two or more kilometres (a mile or more). It is easy to confuse some territorial calls of British owls with hunting calls, since both can be sharp, explosive sounds. When used for hunting, the idea is to scare unsuspecting small mammals into movement.

Owls seem to come in all sizes whilst remaining recognizably owl in shape. The biggest, the Eagle Owls, are fearsome beasts with folded wing lengths of 50cm (20 inches) and wing spans approaching 2 metres (6 feet). The most massive species weigh in at over 4kg (9lb) and are capable of killing fully grown hares or the largest ducks. They are widespread over most of the world but not living as native birds in Britain although there are plenty of one species, the Eagle Owl *Bubo bubo*, in parts of Europe. At the other end of the scale there are such engaging species as the tiny Pygmy Owl *Glaucidium passerinum*, with a wing length of about 10cm (4 inches), considerably less

Eagle Owl.

than a Starling, and a wing span of about 35cm (14 inches). It weighs about 60g (2oz) or so and feeds on small mammals. This species breeds in Central Europe and Scandinavia but has not yet been recorded in the wild in Britain.

The scientists who 'classify' birds have not agreed amongst themselves exactly how many species of owl there are but they do agree that there are two main types of owls. The Tytonidae (Barn Owls) include ten species, and the rest are Strigidae – true owls. The differences are fairly minor, but consistent, and relate to small details of the birds' skeletons: Barn Owls have rather longer legs and smaller eyes than the others. The Barn Owl *Tyto alba* is one of Britain and Ireland's own owls: it is absent only from the northernmost parts of Scotland; it is also present over all but the northern parts of Europe. As its Latin name indicates, it is the 'white owl' and it used to be a familiar sight over much of the country. Sadly its numbers have declined drastically over recent years.

The other four owls common in Britain are all true owls, and belong to three different genera: two of them belong to the genus *Asio* – the open-country Short-eared *Asio flammeus*, which is mostly found in upland areas or coastal marshland and is absent from Ireland, and *Asio otus*, the Long-eared, which is a woodland species widely but thinly distributed throughout Britain and Ireland. Our other woodland species is the Tawny Owl *Strix aluco*. This is the familiar brown owl after whom the Brownie troop leaders are all named and the species which, if any, goes 'twit twhoo'. Finally, since its introduction took place some 100 years ago, we must include the Little Owl *Athene noctua*, which lives in England, much of Wales and southern Scotland. This is rather smaller than the other four species, which are more or less the same size. Little Owls are natives of southern Europe.

Our most spectacular species is the Snowy Owl *Nyctea scandiaca*. This magnificent white owl, almost as big as an Eagle Owl, is really an Arctic or sub-Arctic species which has been seen regularly in northern Scotland for many years. For a few years a pair successfully bred on Fetlar, in the Shetlands, but sadly the females on Shetland have not had a male for many years now.

Every now and again we find in Britain two small European owls: the Tengmalm's *Aegolius funereus* comes across in very small numbers in autumns when owls in Scandinavia and Finland are forced to move about a lot, due to a crash in numbers of small mammals on which they prey. The other is the small-eared Scops Owl *Otus scops*, which sometimes overshoots its southern European breeding grounds on spring migration from its winter quarters in Africa south of the Sahara.

As we shall see, these different species have many things in common but they also have important differences which enable them to survive and keep their separate identities. Many species of owl, in different parts of the world, exploit similar circumstances. For instance, there are several different owls that feed on prey in grassland and some are closely related, for example our Short-eared and the African Marsh Owl *Asio capensis*. They are able to maintain themselves as living, viable species since they are well separated geographically: the furthest south that a Short-eared ever breeds is in France or northern Spain and no African Marsh Owls are now breeding north of the Sahara save a few pairs in Morocco.

Some of the strangest owls, found over much of Africa and southern Asia, are the various different species of fishing owls. They are well adapted to taking fish because they have long legs and specialized scales on the soles of their featherless feet, which grow into sharp spikes to grasp the slippery fish: in fact exactly the same adaptations which have evolved in the Osprey – their equivalent amongst the diurnal birds of prey. They are not well known birds for they are very nocturnal in their habits, but they have been seen feeding by perching beside a river and plunging for fish swimming at or just below the surface. They have neither the facial discs nor the soft silent plumage of terrestrial hunting owls. Some are very large – approaching Eagle Owl size – and they have been seen wading about in shallow water pouncing on small fish and invertebrates. One was even seen feeding on a crocodile carcase, but this was probably just the owl taking advantage of carrion rather than a feat of extreme hunting prowess. Even in Britain Tawny Owls regularly feed on frogs taken at or near water and they have been recorded both taking fish from the water surface and wading in water whilst hunting – one has even been seen hovering over coastal surf.

The handsome Hawk Owl *Surnia ulula* is the Arctic representative, occurring all round the northern parts of Europe, Asia and America, of a rather un-owl-like group of owls. They look like hawks, with powerful wings and fairly long tails and do not have very well developed facial discs. They are basically nocturnal, but hunt by sight and include some very impressive birds. Perhaps the best is the aptly named Powerful Owl *Ninox strenua*, which is found in wooded valleys in south-east Australia. Here it fulfils the role of a big *Strix* species and is actually the largest predatory bird on the whole continent with the exception of the native eagles. It feeds mainly on mammals like possums and gliders but does take some birds.

In America there are Burrowing Owls *Speotyto cunicularia*, which used to be very common birds living in the burrows of prairie dog 'towns'. These have become pretty rare because of determined persecution of prairie dogs

Hawk Owl.

by farmers who saw them as competitors for the grazing and also were
worried about cattle and horses breaking their legs in the holes. The natural
townships held not only the dogs and owls but also plenty of rattle-snakes
and their own mustelid – the now very rare black-footed ferret. There were
stories that all these creatures lived happily together but, of course, the owls,
snakes and ferrets would all prey on the prairie dogs when the opportunity
came up and undoubtedly the ferrets and snakes would not be averse to owl
for tea.

This swift overview of owls cannot finish without a mention of one of the
most endearing species – the Elf Owl *Micrathene whitneyi*, which is only
found in parts of Mexico and the south-western United States. It is a desert
species and most often breeds in woodpecker holes in the huge saguaro

cactus. It lacks ear tufts and is very small, little bigger than a sparrow. As a local bird with specialized requirements it is a particularly prized sighting for many twitchers (dedicated bird spotters—called 'listers' in America) and there are some readily accessible birds, found close to a highway and not in the depth of the desert, which apparently have regular fan clubs. The grateful birders can be found waiting at the particular cactus, binoculars at the ready, to make the all-important tick on their lists.

Evolving owls

The ancestral nocturnal bird, alive 100 million years ago in the Cretaceous period, from which the owls are thought to have evolved, was also the original parent of the present-day nightjars. The first recognizable owls appeared in the fossil record about 60 million years ago in North America. The species has no exact counterpart nowadays but represents a stage in the evolution of owls as we know them today. Within 10-20 million years various further species had evolved with fossils found in several parts of

Great moments in owl evolution: 60 million years ago.

North America (Colorado, Wyoming and California) and Europe (France, England and Germany). By about 20 million years ago there were several species in existence whose fossils have been identified as belonging to the same family as species living today—*Bubo, Asio, Tyto, Otus* and *Strix*.

There is no evidence, from the fossil record, of any of today's species having evolved earlier than the Pleistocene period – starting about 3 million years ago. However there is plenty of evidence from fossils that many species which survived until quite recently, in geological terms, are now extinct. The Barn Owls (Tytonidae) seem to have suffered particularly badly; there are more extinct species recorded than there are live ones now (eight).

It is easy to see why owls have been so successful in evolving different forms to inhabit all sorts of areas from the Tropics to the high Arctic: they have made the night their time and they have been able to develop skills in hunting which give them the unique ability, amongst birds, of preying on other nocturnal vertebrates. After all a mouse is a mouse and a vole a vole whichever continent it happens to live on. The owl's skills will be pitted against the same sort of behaviour patterns in the grasslands of Kenya, the Steppes of Asia and the American Pampas or Prairie.

British owls

What they look like and where you find them

BARN OWL *Tyto alba*
This beautiful bird is the only white owl you are likely to see – Snowy Owls are very rare indeed and most sightings are made in the north of Scotland. The Barn Owl can look pure white when seen flying softly and silently at dusk like a huge moth. However a really good look at the bird shows that it is a mixture of various shades of pale golden-orange with grey and, sometimes, black specklings. British birds are noticeably lighter on their fronts than the Barn Owls further north and east in Europe – ours belong to the race *Tyto alba alba*, known as the White-breasted Barn Owl, the darker ones being *T. a. guttata* (Dark-breasted). Barn Owls are widely distributed round the world with races of the same species over much of North and South America, Africa, Arabia, India and South-east Asia and Australia.

Barn Owls are medium-sized owls without ear tufts, and are well-nigh unmistakeable for any other species. The wing span is about 90cm (35

inches) and the average weight of males just about 300g (11oz), with females, although they are not significantly bigger in wing length or other measurements, generally a bit heavier.

The Barn Owl is most often seen in flight, quartering the ground at a height of 2 to 5 metres (6 to 15 feet), ready, instantly, to drop on any prey which shows itself. These very regular patrols may be punctuated by short rests on useful perches, such as fence posts, from which prey may sometimes be caught. Barn Owls are not birds of woodland but they do not mind a few trees and bushes scattered over their hunting area. This will usually be open permanent pasture or moorland with a good population of small mammals. Dense, tall ground vegetation is shunned.

Breeding Barn Owls very often choose to nest in buildings, hence the name. Nowadays the typical site is probably in the roof-space of a disused farmhouse in a moorland area but they readily take to nest-boxes – usually placed in roofs of buildings – and will inhabit used farm buildings or substantial tree holes. Their preference is generally for a fairly commodious site and they will seldom nest in cramped surroundings. Often, when they are nesting in buildings, the actual nest will be put far inside the building; nest-boxes should also be large and put deep in the building.

Although they are apparently conspicuous birds, many Barn Owls live in our countryside without being seen by bird-watchers. Often they live in perfectly ordinary areas on the outskirts of villages or by farm buildings where no other species attract the watcher's attention. Their calls include a variety of shrieks and yells and also softer snoring, purring, hissing and wheezing noises. Recently their numbers declined considerably when persistent pesticides were in use. They are now so rare that they have special protection under Schedule 1 of the Wildlife and Countryside Act (1981).

SNOWY OWL *Nyctea scandiaca*
This is both the biggest and the rarest of Britain's owls. Indeed it can be claimed as a British owl only because of the birds which bred on Fetlar (Shetland) for the few years from 1967 to 1975. The adult male looks wholly white or pale cream but youngsters and females are more or less strongly barred and spotted with dark brown or grey. In flight they look rather like albino Common Buzzards; on the ground they may perch fully upright, bent forwards or resting horizontally. They are said to resemble large white cats and have been called 'cat birds' in various dialects. They are very big. Wing span averages about 150cm (59 inches), with females quite a bit bigger than

Barn Owl with chicks.

(Above) *Male Snowy Owl and prey;* (opposite) *Little Owl.*

males. Their weights are a bit less than 2kg (4½lb) for the male and a bit more for the female. Their eyes are lemon-yellow at most ages.

Snowy Owls generally inhabit the Arctic tundra, mainly the lands bordering the Arctic Ocean. At irregular intervals there are 'irruptions': when the small mammals they eat crash in numbers, and the birds travel much further south than usual; most come southwards every winter in response to the harshness of the winters in their breeding grounds. They are superbly adapted to the cold and can sit out truly appalling weather conditions in the lee of a rock. Often they will feed by flying at prey from such a perch; sometimes they will quarter the ground or even hover, and they have also been seen chasing small mammals on foot. The nest is a simple scrape on a raised area so that the incubating bird has a good view. The Shetland breeding birds were probably a result of an irruption in the mid-1960s. Several females are still in the area but no male has joined them for many years. A frustrated set of old maids waiting patiently (?) for the next irruption. Some may well still be around even if the next eligible bachelor does not appear until the next century.

LITTLE OWL *Athene noctua*
This is our smallest breeding owl. It is rather flat-headed in appearance with no ear tufts. It is overall brown in colour with pale and white blotches and

spots, including rather glowering eyebrows. The eyes are clear yellow. This owl is very often seen perched on a roadside fence post or telegraph pole at dusk or dawn. Its wing span is about 55cm (22 inches) and weight about 170g (6oz), with females a little heavier than males in general.

Since they mostly feed on large insects, earthworms and other invertebrates, Little Owls often take their prey directly from a perch. The characteristic call – *Keyoo* – has been a feature of the British countryside for only a hundred years: the species was deliberately introduced to add variety to our avifauna several times in the last few years of the nineteenth century and had become well established by the 1920s. Despite a very bad reputation with gamekeepers for being ferocious killers of Pheasant poults, Little Owls could be found all over England and Wales and into southern Scotland by the start of the Second World War.

Breeding Little Owls can be found in all sorts of holes and crevices. Usually these are in trees, sometimes in nest-boxes but also in rocks or even buildings. They are not owls of true woodland but rather prefer parkland or well hedged farmland areas over most of Britain. Little Owls can be found all over much of Europe, apart from Norway, Sweden and Finland, and across Asia to northern Korea. They also breed over much of northern Africa and most of Turkey. Related species include the Burrowing Owl of the Americas.

TAWNY OWL   *Strix aluco*
This is our best-known owl. The Tawny Owl is tawny – a definitely brown owl – soft, fluffy, big-headed and without ear tufts. There are two different colour forms, of which the brown one is by far the commonest in Britain. Its plumage is very richly patterned and coloured, with individual feathers decorated with complicated designs giving an overall mottled effect. A rare colour form is basically grey rather than brown. The eyes are dark at all ages.

The Tawny is our biggest common owl, although its wing span of about 100cm (39 inches) is probably a little shorter than the average Short-eared; overall it is a bulkier bird. Tawny weights average about 400g (14oz) for the males and 590g (21oz) for the females. The biggest on record have been females weighing in at over 700g (25oz). It is the Tawny that hoots with a double syllable, *Toowhit-twhoo*, as well as a huge variety of other sounds. The alarm *Keewick* is often heard but is quite similar to other species' calls under the same circumstances. The Tawny Owl is a woodland owl, making its living from small mammals and birds, large insects and frogs – all sorts of prey – found in its own exclusive territory; the owl wins its territory within a few months of hatching and keeps it throughout its life. Prey is detected from a perch and the kill is made after a quick swoop downwards. For a Tawny Owl woodland may mean the ancient forests of Hampshire or the pine woods of Scotland. It is equally at home in spinneys on farmland, in newly planted conifers, in mature gardens or even urban parkland. It can be found over almost the whole of Britain – except treeless areas – but has never reached Ireland as a breeding bird. It is found over most of central and southern Europe and also across central Asia into China. Related species are even more widely distributed.

LONG-EARED OWL *Asio otus*

The Long-eared Owl (as you might expect) has very long ears. Its plumage is rather greyer than that of a Tawny Owl and the ears and brilliant orange eyes, if you can see it well, will give away its identity. The individual breast feathers are both barred and streaked giving a characteristic pattern. In flight, in daylight, it can be confused with the Short-eared Owl for it too has a dark carpal patch (halfway up the leading edge of the underside of the wing), but the Long-eared is greyer overall and the Short-eared is more of a buff colour and has longer wings.

The wing span of the Long-eared is roughly 95cm (37 inches) and the weight averages 250-300g (11oz). One of its territorial calls is a characteristic series of pure hoots but it has a varied suite of calls during the breeding season; as with the Short-eared (see over) wing-claps are also used.

Long-eared owls breed in woodland, but will make do with small clumps of trees. During the winter they can often be found in scrubland areas – sometimes several birds together in communal roosts. The more usual roost site is on a branch close to the trunk of a tree. Long-eared Owls may sometimes be seen quartering the ground like Barn or Short-eared Owls at dawn or dusk but they are generally a very nocturnal species. Long-eared Owls breed over much of Europe, northern Asia and North America. During the winter the northernmost birds move south and good numbers of migrants reach Britain from Finland and Scandinavia.

SHORT-EARED OWL *Asio flammeus*

This is the owl of open country and a characteristic bird of many of Britain's mountain and moorland areas. Overall it is buff-coloured, blotched with darker brown. The underwing has a distinctive dark carpal patch and the wing tips are also dark. The facial disc is pale, but ringed by darker feathers, and it has lemon-yellow eyes set in small patches of dark feathers. Young birds are rather darker and, on average, males are paler than females.

Short-eared Owl, short-tailed vole!

The wing span can reach 110cm (43 inches) but the Short-eared is considerably less bulky than the Tawny Owl, with an average weigh of about 350g (12oz). Females, as is the case with most owls, weigh rather more than males. Its most characteristic sound is the wing-clapping given in aerial display in bursts of up to half a dozen claps. These bursts can be repeated time after time, probably for advertisement and territorial display.

Short-eared Owls do not only hunt by night: foraging birds can be seen flying over open ground throughout the day. Their long wings give them a bouncy, buoyant and effortless flight and they seem to be tireless and very

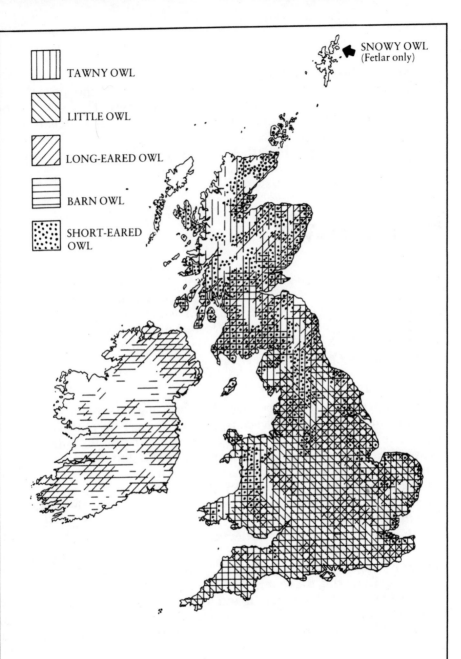

SNOWY OWL
(Fetlar only)

TAWNY OWL

LITTLE OWL

LONG-EARED OWL

BARN OWL

SHORT-EARED OWL

Approximate distribution of five British species.

methodical in their searching for prey. Open moorland and coastal marshes are the natural habitats with which one associates them but they do very well in young conifer plantations before the canopy closes. They nest on the ground, often in a tussock of grass, and closely regulate their clutch to match the available food (see p. 75). Short-eared Owls are found round north-east Europe, northern Asia and North America with varieties in southern South America and even on the Falklands.

Euro-owls

Apart from the six species of owls which either breed now or have recently bred in Britain, there are a further seven species that can truly be called Europeans. Some are rare visitors to Britain and others may be encountered on holiday – even by the non-birder. The bell-like chimes of Scops Owls are characteristic of a Mediterranean summer night and not a little disconcerting if you do not know what they are.

SCOPS OWL   *Otus scops*
This is a super little-eared owl of overall greyish or even sandy colour with a very intricate and delicate brown and grey patterning. Paler marks form lines on the back between the closed wings. The eyes are yellow. With luck the roosting bird can be spotted in a bush or tree, motionless during the day and trying its best to look like a dead branch – and it does. Scops is a very small owl with a wing span of between 55 (22in) and 60cm(24in) and it weighs about 90g (4oz). The territorial call is a very sweet, clear and bell-like hoot. Birds that live next-door to each other will adjust their calls so that they each have their own note. The interval between calls is different from bird to bird; they will call between once every two and once every three seconds. A quiet olive grove may have five or six within earshot and they sound like a distant chime of bells ringing the changes.

Scops Owl is mainly nocturnal and lives in open woods, scrubland and parkland found over much of southern Europe and through parts of southern Russia well into Asia. They eat mostly invertebrate food, including earthworms when available, but they are able to catch small mammals and birds. Like the Little Owl, Scops generally hunt from a perch. A few winter in the Mediterranean but the major part of the population migrates south of the Sahara into the more wooded areas south of the Sahel and even into

Scops Owl: this is what cryptic camouflage means.

Kenya. Most British records are of calling birds overshooting their breeding grounds and reaching us in spring.

EAGLE OWL *Bubo bubo*

This is an extraordinarily impressive bird: an unmistakeable, massive-eared owl best described as 'barrel-shaped'. The birds from temperate and northern areas are strongly marked dark brown birds with gleaming orange eyes. The southern birds from desert and dry areas are paler in overall colour and have yellow eyes.

The wing span of females regularly exceeds 180cm (71 inches) and males are about 10% smaller on average. Weights range from 1500g (3lb 5oz) for a small, thin male to 4000g (8lb 13oz) for a large, fit and flourishing northern female. The male's advertising call, which announces possession of its territory, suits the bird and is a deep, throaty and reverberating *Ooohuh* repeated six or seven times a minute; it can be heard over distances of two or three kilometres (a mile or two) on a quiet night.

There are signs that although really birds of the wilderness they are becoming more used to man and there are now many records of them breeding at rubbish dumps – a good source of rats – in Finland. Almost anything that moves is fair game for this hunter and roe deer, lambs and calves are recorded as having been eaten. It seems likely that these were sick or already dead when taken but large birds such as Grey Heron and Capercaillie are certainly killed as are pet cats and dogs. Some are expert at fishing and large fish up to 1500g (3lb 5oz) have been found in their nests.

Rarely does a straggler come to Britain, although a pair has recently reared a chick successfully. In Europe the Eagle Owl is missing from many areas of high human population but it breeds all the way across Asia to the Pacific. Similar and very closely related species are to be found over much of the rest of the world.

HAWK OWL *Surnia ulula*

This is a rather strange owl with, as its name suggests, a resemblance to a hawk. It has a small head with a prominent dark arc along the outer edge of each pale facial disc. The Hawk Owl's tail is much longer and more conspicuous than those of most other owls. Its colour is predominantly grey with a pale nape of neck and shoulders and pale underparts strongly barred with black. The eyes are yellow. It will often perch very conspicuously on the topmost branch of a tree or the highest point of a telegraph pole.

The wing span is between 75 and 80cm (30 inches and 32 inches) and weight about 300g (11oz) (rather more for the female). This makes it comparable in size, as well as shape, to a female Sparrowhawk but with a slightly bigger wing span. The main advertising call of the male is a long, rolling *Hoo hoo hoo ooooooooooo* which may last for up to 8 or 10 seconds.

Hawk Owls live in Arctic woodland and their range extends northwards to the treeline: they breed all round the North Pole – in Europe, Asia and North America. They hunt by day from perches or from a hover – like a Kestrel – to feed on small mammals. When the prey population crashes, wandering Hawk Owls are seen much further south than their usual breeding range; the few records of Hawk Owls in Britain have occurred when there has been a shortage of prey in their usual haunts.

PYGMY OWL *Glaucidium passerinum*
This tiny, soft grey owl has pale, spotted and barred underparts and a buff-grey back with pale markings. The pale eyebrows curve downwards towards the edges of the bill. Its eyes are a pale yellow. It may sometimes perch with its tail half-cocked and will even flick it about rather like a shrike or flycatcher.

Once you can see its true size, there can be no doubt about its identity. Its wing span is about 35cm (14 inches) some two-thirds the size of the similar, earless Little Owl. In fact it is not much bigger than a Crossbill or Hawfinch. Average weights vary between 60 and 75g (2 and 3oz). The advertising call is similar to that of a speeded-up Scops Owl with 45 to 50 hoots per minute.

Pygmy Owl and Siskin prey.

The Pygmy Owl lives in northern Europe and Asia, with some still present in the mountains of central Europe. During the breeding season it is most often to be found in coniferous woodland where it will take to nest-boxes. In winter it may move into deciduous woods. It hunts mainly in twilight for small mammals and will usually drop on them from a hunting perch. It has yet to be recorded in the wild in Britain.

URAL OWL   *Strix uralensis*

This is a bigger, greyer and longer-tailed version of the Tawny Owl. There is a brown wash over the wings and back but it is not as bright as most Tawny Owls. The facial disc is grey and the eyes dark. The underparts are heavily streaked with dark, almost black, marks. The tail is fairly strong and long with a wedge-shaped tip and half a dozen dark bars across it.

Ural Owl.

Wing span reaches about 130cm (51 inches) and the weight of a male is about 600g (1lb 4oz) and that of a female 800g (1lb 12oz) even 1,000g (2lb 3oz) sometimes. The territorial call is a very characteristic *Who-ooo whoo Hoo-OOO-hoo* and may be repeated time after time.

The Ural Owl mainly inhabits forests in north-eastern Europe and northern Asia although there are a few outlying populations further south. In some areas deciduous woodland is preferred and in others conifers. However birds may also breed in more open areas, even on farmland and near human habitation. Prey taken includes small mammals and birds up to the size of Woodpigeon. The Ural Owl is a fairly sedentary species, not so far reported in Britain and unlikely to reach us.

Great Grey Owl.

GREAT GREY OWL   *Strix nebulosa*
The Great Grey Owl is just that. Almost as long but not so bulky as an Eagle Owl, it is a very impressive bird. It seems to have a big head with well developed facial discs including concentric darker rings on a grey background. The yellow eyes are separated from the bill by semi-circular, upright eyebrows which almost join with pale moustachial stripes. The back is overall grey with darker streaks, stripes and other patterning. The underparts are streaked with dark grey and the throat and breast feathers are also barred.

The wings are long and the wing span may reach 150cm (59 inches) or more. Weights of males average about 900g (2lb) and females 1200g (2lb 10oz); a female has been recorded at 1900g (4lb 3oz). The territorial call is a very deep boom, lacking the complicated phrasing of the Ural Owl.

Although they are undoubtedly woodland owls, Great Greys often hunt in relatively open country and during the day. Their diet is pretty well restricted to voles and these are even hunted under the snow with the owl plunging into it, feet or even face first, to get at the unfortunate animal underneath. In winters when the vole populations are low Great Grey Owls may be forced south from their northern breeding areas – around the North Pole in Europe, Asia and North America. However there are no records in Britain and this is another species unlikely to reach us under its own steam.

TENGMALM'S OWL *Aegolius funereus*
This owl is about the size of a Little but with a much bigger head and more strongly marked facial feathers. The eyes are yellow. The dark edges to the facial disc are reminiscent of a Hawk Owl and the 'raised eyebrows' give it a rather surprised look. Apart from the head and a slightly longer tail, the rest of its structure and colour is very like a Little Owl.

Wing span may reach about 60cm (24 inches) and weights vary from 90g (3oz) to 170g (6oz) depending on the time of year and sex of the bird. The call is a very regular short hoot *Po-po-po-po-po-po-po-po*, which can be audible over a long distance. The first call of a series may contain 10 or 15 *pos* but subsequent ones will be half that number.

This is another northern species breeding round North America, Asia and Europe. Some isolated populations nest in central and southern Europe. Small mammals are most often eaten but birds are sometimes an important part of the diet. Tengmalm's is a woodland bird, but will hunt in all sorts of habitats. In years when mammal populations fail it will move considerable distances southwards and may then reach Britain, but irregularly and in very small numbers.

Tengmalm's Owl.

Scops scoop

On a visit to Majorca I recorded a
'Living World' radio programme
for the BBC. We recorded, as a part
of it, an item about Scops Owls
surreptitiously taped one night just
beside a military camp close to
Puerto Pollencia in the north of the
island. Two close Scops were
calling to each other beautifully,
with another in the background,
and we managed to finish the
recording without any traffic noise
—and before the sentry rounded
the large building he was guarding

to spoil it with his echoing footsteps. John Harrison, the producer, used this, as intended, as the final sequence of the programme which faded out to the bell-like and absolutely characteristic notes of the calling Scops.

Soon after the programme was broadcast a Scops Owl, overshooting on spring migration, was heard chiming in a garden on the Hampshire/Surrey border. I believe that this bird was reported to a bird-watcher by an interested member of the public and was not found by an expert. I like to think that it was a result of the memorable ending to the broadcast that this rare visitor was found and recognized. It stayed around for a good long time and was heard (not, I think, often seen) by lots of delighted bird-watchers.

Sound pictures

One of the most amazing adaptations that has developed in the owls to help them in their nocturnal existence is their 'ear-sight'. It would be something of an insult merely to describe their ability as hearing. It is, of course, best developed in the truly nocturnal species rather than in those that rely more on their eyesight at dawn and dusk or during the day. Indeed a comparison of the species which have been studied in detail indicates that it is a feature of temperate and boreal owls and not of sub-tropical and tropical ones. The advantages of 'ear-sight' are lost in the noisy tropics; there would be little point in the tropical species developing a method of hunting that depended on being able to localize the tiny sounds made by their prey; they would be hunting in the cacophony of a tropical night – cicadas, crickets, frogs and all squeaking, strumming, clicking and croaking away nineteen to the dozen, drowning out any tiny sounds made by the small and furry brigade.

As hunters in an Arctic forest, silent but for the moaning of the wind in the tops of the trees and the faint rustles of mice, voles and shrews in the litter, owls have developed audio apparatus capable of pinpointing their prey so precisely that several species can strike and kill in complete darkness. We have grown accustomed to the idea of bats using echo-location and it is also undoubtedly used by some birds (for instance, the Oilbird which lives in the caves of tropical America) – but this is quite different from what owls do. Their fantastic powers come from hearing the noises made by their prey, rather than emitting their own sounds. Strangely, owl ears are only slightly more sensitive than our own. This may seem well-nigh impossible: for humans have a rather poor sense of direction and distance if they close their eyes and use ears alone. However, the blind are able to make out the distance and direction from which a sound originates very much more accurately than can the rest of the population, who habitually use their eyes, because they have to rely on developing their hearing. And this is using human ears, which are set symmetrically on each side of our heads and have the same frequency response. Owls have all sorts of tricks available to them which, in combination, enable the most skilled to accomplish seemingly impossible feats.

First is the facial disc of loose feathers with thick, stiff ones lining its edges which acts as a wave-guide – or hearing trumpet – for each ear. The loose inner feathers have very little substance to attenuate the sound waves passing through them. The stiff feathers of the facial disc act just like a human's cupped hand, placed behind the ear, to collect and amplify faint sounds. The bird's ruff of stiff feathers may even be mobile and, controlled by special muscles, enable the bird to alter its focus at will. Certainly the amplification and localization provided is very important. Experiments in captive conditions have shown that an owl, which was perfectly capable of catching a mouse when tested earlier, failed to strike accurately when its disc feathers were plucked.

The ruff of feathers is often itself slightly asymmetrical but in many species the openings in the skin to the ears and, with several species, the whole shape of the ear cavities in the skull differ from one side to the other. The maximum difference may be an ear opening 15° further up the skull than the other; as well as this, in front of the ear opening there is a flap of skin which the bird can control and erect to act like a much smaller cupped hand *in front of* the ear. This clearly serves further to concentrate the sound focused forwards by the ruff of feathers.

The ear structure, in the species showing marked asymmetry, is often different too. Tests have been done with some such species which show that one ear hears particular frequencies better than the other. Of course the ear apparatus is very well developed in the nocturnal species, which have not only very large eardrums but also lots of nerve cells in the auditory part of the brain. A well known comparison gives a count of 95,000 neurons in the auditory area of a Barn Owl's brain compared with only 27,000 in a diurnal crow (which weighs twice as much as an owl).

All sorts of experiments have been done to find out exactly how owls use their ears to 'see' their prey. One of the most famous series was carried out by Roger Payne at Cornell University almost twenty years ago. He used a

captive Barn Owl in a large light-proof room and was able to show that a mouse could be caught, not invariably, but much more often than not, in *total* darkness, provided it either had a leaf stuck to its tail or was running about in dry leaves. In other words, the owl was definitely able to hear where it was. The owls tested did not strike as quickly when there was no light but Payne felt that this was probably because they did not want to collide with anything solid.

He then tested the owls not with a mouse but with loudspeakers which played mouse-rustlings under the sandy floor of the room. He arranged it so that the speaker was turned off as the owl left its perch but, because of the sand covering, he was able to assess, from the marks the owl's claws had left, whether the strike would have hit a mouse where the loudspeaker was or not. The results showed that relatively high frequencies were being used by the owl (over 8,500hz) and that if all sounds over 5,000hz were filtered out the owl would not have a go at all. The owl had to be within 7 metres of the rustle for it to make a hunting foray and almost always a successful strike resulted.

All this sounds pretty fantastic. What he then found out was even more amazing. By pulling a dead mouse with a leaf attached to its tail around the room, he recorded over 200 hits and some 5 misses – the average miss was out by very much less than a degree in the direction taken from the perch. Watch out Eric Bristow! Put into human terms, the Barn Owl would be able to score a double top at darts just about every time – provided double top rustled. Even with the loudspeaker tests, where over half the attempts were misses, the owl averaged only 2.9° out horizontally and 2.5° in the vertical plane.

So how do they do it? The answer seems to be very simple. The owl can hear a rustle in one ear much louder than in the other, unless it is pointing directly at the noise; the ability to isolate sounds depends on a 15° difference vertically between the siting of the ears. It is much easier to perceive that the sound in one ear is getting louder (or softer) as the other gets softer (or louder) than simply – as we have to – trying to find the peak noise. The owl is able to use 'positive feedback' from both ears to make its judgment and so reaches standards of accuracy unattainable by humans with much the same sort of hearing potential. So all the owl has to do, when it hears a rustle, is to turn its head so that the loudness of that rustle is the same in each ear *and* as loud as possible. As soon as it has done this its head is pointing directly at its prey. Cine shots have shown that the striking Barn Owl seems to be looking directly at its prey, even in pitch dark, just before it strikes. Thus the point of aim of both the bird's ears and its eyes are the same – as one would expect. At the last moment the owl brings back its head and the talons are thrust forward – open and fully armed – and the vole's cookie has well and truly crumbled a fraction of a second later.

Although this ability to see by hearing is highly developed in many owls they are, of course, very well able to use their eyesight when there is available light. The exact coincidence of the eye and ear aiming point indicates how easy it is for them to combine sight and sound when hunting. However there are many nights each winter in the northern wilderness, far from any street lights, when complete cloud cover prevents the birds from feeding by sight alone throughout the long night. It is then that hearing comes into its own. Eyesight can also be helpful if the wind is rustling fallen leaves and giving out false sound clues. And in good daylight hearing may be essential to pick out the sounds of small mammals when the prey is running around under snow cover. It has even been suggested that this is why the Great Grey Owl is so large – simply to allow it to break instantaneously through the snow cover onto the rustling meal below.

It is also very important, for the owl's survival, that any hunting using sound alone during complete darkness should be done in an area that the bird knows really well. Without being able to see large and dangerous inanimate objects, like trees, branches, wires, rocks and buildings, collisions would be common, since the owls are not themselves emitting any sound. The flying bird would have no chance of avoiding them. By staying within a well known territory, the sensible owl can remember where such dangerous accidents might happen and still have a chance to feed from a safe and familiar perch.

Owl talk

Many people think that birds talk to each other – and so they do – but not in sentences. When owls call the calls have a meaning both for the immediate family of the calling bird and also for other owls. Within the pair it is a means of knowing where your partner is and reassuring him (or her) that all is well. Before pairing has taken place the call of the territorial male also serves to attract a female but, later, it becomes a declaration of ownership pure and simple. The male, coming back to the nest with prey, will call to warn the female that he is coming for she might otherwise attack first, to defend the eggs or nestlings, and ask who it is afterwards.

The youngsters must appease the parent's instinct to eat small furry things when, soon after they have emerged from the egg, they are themselves small

and apparently furry. They also need to indicate hunger to their parents – fetch more food *now*! Later, when they have left the nest but are still being fed, their parents will use the call of the young to find where they are hiding and have, themselves, calls which will provoke the chicks into calling and giving away their hiding place.

Many owls also have explosive hunting calls—very loud, sharp calls which are apparently given by the bird whilst it is hunting. Various theories have been put forward as to what this is for but the best explanation seems to be that it is to provoke small mammals into a sudden movement. This the owl may see, or hear, and so the call may be a real hunting aid.

Seeing in the dark

No, of course they can't. Owls' eyes work just like yours or mine and it is an absolute impossibility that they should work where there is no light at all. Only when a photon strikes a receptor in the retina and a message is passed to the visual cortex of the owl's brain can it be said to 'see'. Still, the eyes of some nocturnal owls have evolved just about as far as possible in being able to detect and make sense of the lowest light levels.

The eyes of mammals and birds are very similar indeed. The external light which falls on the eye is focused using a lens (this is the pupil) on receptors covering the back of the eyeball. Muscles attached to the lens enable its shape to be changed at will so that the light from objects at different distances from the eye can be focused on the receptors. In a healthy human eye the range of focus is from roughly 10cm (4 inches) to infinity, but this might be reduced to between 5cm and 10cm (2 to 4 inches) in someone who was severely short-sighted. An owl in this condition, without the human's ability to purchase spectacles or contact lenses, would not survive to kill its first mouse.

We are used to turning our heads to look straight at something in which we are interested, but we can also rotate the eyeballs in our heads to look from side to side. Our eyes work together all the time and we have a good three-dimensional sense because each eye produces an image which is slightly different from the other and our brains can interpret those differences to allow us to assess the distance, size, movement, etc, of the object we are looking at. Owls have eyes which work together and give a good extent of binocular vision, but the structure of each eye is more tubular

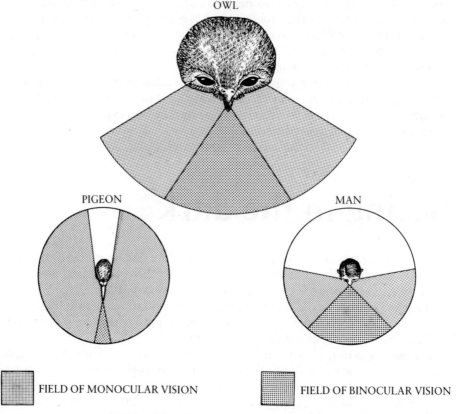

PIGEON

MAN

▨ FIELD OF MONOCULAR VISION

▨ FIELD OF BINOCULAR VISION

Fields of vision of an owl, pigeon and man.

than round. This means that each eye is really rather like a small telescope fixed in the skull and so the owl is only able to get the binocular effect when it is looking directly at the object it wants to see. Other kinds of bird have some control over the direction in which their eyes are pointing but to a much lesser extent that we have. For the owls this has put a premium on supple necks so that some species can rotate their heads through almost 360° where a human can manage much less than 180°.

By developing tubular eyes pointing forwards the owls have ensured that they have an exceptionally good arc of binocular vision – where the distance and movement of prey can be exactly determined. Most birds have their eyes prominently stuck on the sides of their heads so that they only have a small arc of binocular vision immediately to the front but a very wide field above, to the side and even behind. For those who are hunted, this is a very useful adaptation, as they will have a good chance of seeing a predator before they feel its talons. For the hunter the overriding need is for efficiency in attack rather than good defence.

The iris of an owl's eye can open very wide in dark conditions to allow as much light as possible to enter. If we were able to see the owl's eye in conditions of really poor light there would be rather little of the beautiful yellows and oranges shown by several species, for the iris would be fully open and the pupil large. In bright conditions the major part of the exposed area of the eye of the same species glows yellow or orange. The back of the eye is rather flattened and packed with receptors – mostly rods which are the type concerned with seeing in poor light conditions. There are also some cones present and so owls are capable of seeing colour in daylight. Although this decreases the detail they can discern, the owl's rods are grouped together so that several feed into one nerve cell communicating with the brain. Lack of detail in what they see, which results from this grouping of rods, is less important to the birds than the increased ability to pick out objects in poor light conditions, the benefit of having several receptors feeding into one nerve cell.

This sensitivity to the tiniest amount of light reaching the eye is the feature

Dazzle

Since owls have eyes which are adapted for the best possible night-time vision, they are big with huge pupils. Not surprisingly there is a very real problem for owls in unexpected bright lights. Perfectly healthy owls are sometimes found on or beside roads and, if you stop the car with the headlights still on and shining at the bird, you can go up to it and pick it up. Your approach will be masked by the bright light. If you keep the bird in the dark for 15 minutes or so it will recover its night vision and fly – provided you do not again shine a bright light at it.

Of course owls can see perfectly well in daylight, or even by the light of bright lights, once their eyes have adapted. There are many records of Tawny and other owls circling light-houses and taking migrants, attracted to the light, from the beams. The owls rely on the fact that their eyes have adapted to the brightness – whereas the other birds' have not – and they would, just like the dazzled owl, have to be kept in a dark box for 15 minutes to be able to adapt to the darkness away from the lighthouse.

for which the truly nocturnal owl's eyes are adapted in every way. The size of the eye, the almost complete opening of the iris, the packing of rods together so densely on the retina and the bundling together of the signals from adjacent rods into one nerve cell all point to this. So just how good are their eyes? This has been tested in experiments like those described on page 34 for testing the ability of Barn Owls to hear. The results are pretty impressive. Barn Owls can detect objects with a surface brilliance a hundredth of what a man can see. Tawny Owls can apparently see dead prey in illuminations of what is described technically as 0.00000016 foot candles, but means pitch black to a research worker, who needed 0.000075 foot candles. This sort of performance is probably good enough to allow a Tawny Owl, in its familiar territory, to fly around on the darkest night and still be able to see the trees and not crash into them. It would probably not be good enough for flying around under the leaf-canopy on a totally overcast night in the autumn but, however dark the night, there are always the hours of dawn and dusk for feeding. Further experiments have shown that not all owls are so good as Tawnies; whilst Long-eared and Ural Owls seem to be almost as good, the same research worker (a Swede by the name of Lindblad) found that Tengmalm's was only ten times better than man and the Pygmy Owl he tested needed twice as much light as he did himself to see a dead mouse.

For a long time it was not appreciated that eyes could be this efficient. It used to be thought that owls were able to see in the infra-red part of the spectrum and so see their prey on the woodland floor as glowing blobs of body-heat. Extensive tests have now proved that they can only see in the ordinary visual part of the spectrum. It was also thought that they were blind in the day. Certainly owls surprised in daylight often look a bit 'owlish' and sleepy but then they are active during the night and need their beauty sleep. Their eyesight in daylight is excellent and they can certainly see colours – though possibly not as well as mammals.

It is important to realize how vital eyesight is to owls. Their hearing can enable them to pounce on prey from a familiar perch. However, they cannot get to know the perch and its surroundings unless they are able to see them when it is light – hearing can only be a supplement and not a substitute for sight. Indeed an owl watched for 14 months that was blind in one eye was barely able to survive and was a noticeably poor hunter. In owls the third eyelid, which sweeps sideways across the eye (the nictitating membrane), is a defence mechanism used to shield the eye from danger at the final strike on prey and during other operations when damage might occur. It is opaque and quite strong, certainly as compared with the transparent membrane of many species who use it simply to clean the surface of the cornea.

Finally one must mention a serious defect which has come about because of the specialized development for seeing in the dark: that is, the owls seem to have developed terminal tunnel vision, and find it difficult to distinguish shapes and identify sources of danger that are not moving with respect to themselves. Derek Bunn describes a Barn Owl at its nest that completely failed to realize that a human was present when he stood still. He found this very useful for he could simply sit still in a chair beside the nest and the bird would not be at all worried. Other people, standing or sitting still outside in the dusk, have had the amazing experience of having a hunting owl decide that the top of their head would make a good perch – a bit painful if you are not in the habit of wearing a hat.

Owls certainly seem to appreciate this problem and often move their heads from side to side, up and down, round and round – or even tilt them so that one eye is above the other (like a member of the Question of Sport team given a photo of someone standing on their head to identify). Just this slight alteration of viewpoint will give further information on the shape and range of the object being inspected.

Keeping it quiet

The extraordinary development of the owl's hearing would be useless in flight if the owl itself had coarse, stiff plumage that rattled and vibrated in flight: the whole point is that the owl is silent so that it can listen for prey. Some flying birds are very noisy and have even developed special feathers that groan, whistle or thrum during display. Not so the owls, particularly the nocturnal ones, for they have very soft plumage which enables them to fly and glide noiselessly when they want to. Several species do actually clap their wings together sharply during display, to make a loud cracking sound, even though their normal flight is silent.

Silent flight is all to do with the overall softness of the plumage. An owl in the hand is amazingly soft and fluffy – so much so that there seems to be hardly any flesh and bone within. Potentially the noisiest feathers are at the leading edges of the wings, since these are the ones which have to cut through the air in forward flight as well as when the wings are beating up and down. With many owls the leading edge of the longest primary (big flight feather) has delicately curved barbs on it. This seems to be a great help in silencing the feather. If you take one of these feathers from an owl and a similarly sized leading flight feather from the wing of a duck (for instance) and beat them through the air at the same rate, the owl's feather is silent but the duck's will whistle and moan.

It is interesting that fishing owls have a much harsher and less soft plumage than the terrestrial and avian feeders. The fish under the surface of the water do not themselves make noises that the owl could hear, so silent flight would not help the hunting owl. It is also likely that the softer plumage would be less waterproof than the denser feathers the fishing owls have developed.

Of course silent flight not only helps in hunting by enabling the owl to hear sounds of its prey. It also ensures that the unfortunate prey hears no sound from the swooping owl that will warn it to make a sudden dash for safety at the last moment.

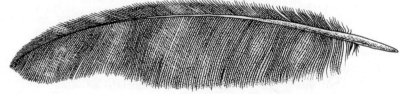

Longest primary feather of Tawny showing 'fluffy' leading edge.

Feet are for killing

By far the most important weapon an owl has is its talons. These are its killing tools and the means of capturing its prey. All owls have very strong feet, with razor-sharp curved toes. In most species these are set on a couple of strong, relatively short, legs. Many species have feathers on their legs, for the birds spend a long time standing around in the cold darkness waiting for prey to come along and these feathers, sometimes extending to the toes, help to minimize heat loss.

Tawny Owl foot.

Most prey is taken by the bird swooping from a perch or from a quartering flight onto it. In all instances the prey is struck with the feet pushed out in front of the bird and the talons open to their fullest extent. This gives the greatest possible area of strike – just as our hands would do if extended to the front with thumb to thumb, forefinger to forefinger. Any mouse or vole unfortunate enough to be within this canopy of claws will be very lucky to escape with its life.

As the prey is struck, the owl's momentum is transferred to the victim – so death may be instantaneous. Even if not, the contact with the prey (or the ground) will cause the talons to be clenched, as the legs are flexed on impact, and so the prey is pulled, even if it has only been struck by a single claw, into a vicious grasp. If the unfortunate animal is still alive, a swift nip from the owl's bill will finish it off.

The efficiency of the owl's talons can be vouched for by many bird ringers who have been unfortunate enough to be 'had' by an owl. Even a Little can do considerable damage and the bird's tenacity is awe-inspiring. Often it is best to wait for the bird to decide to let go rather than trying to lever out the talons. It is particularly painful when the owl's claw pierces a finger joint;

this can severely incapacitate the unfortunate human for a week or more.

One one occasion in Texas I had a Barred Owl, the big *Strix* of the local woodland (in this case about twice the size of a Tawny), hanging from my left wrist and forearm by its very substantial talons. My companion had brought the bird back from the nets and I had started to take it from him when, due to a misunderstanding, he let the bird's feet go. I was determined not to let this superb owl get away and it seemed to think the same about me. I had to be careful not to let my blood drip onto its plumage because it might not have found it too easy to preen away. I was having to hold the bird with my right hand to stop it from escaping and this meant that the huge Texan swamp mosquitoes had a field day on my exposed skin. We tried to lever the owl's claws out of my flesh but it was simply too strong for us and we feared that we might damage the bird if we tried harder. Luckily it did eventually decide to shift its grip and I was able to get it off after the longest forty minutes I can remember spending.

Pellets

This really brings up the question of food.

No, please ignore that as an opening and let's start again.

To the interested bird-watcher the owl's digestive system is a godsend. Although owls are mostly active in the dark, it is quite possible, with many species, to find out exactly what they have been eating in the comfort of one's home by examining the food remains in the pellets that they regurgitate. There is nothing unnatural in the coughing up of pellets – many birds do it, including waders, Kingfishers, Rooks, Robins and birds of prey. Owls have a physical barrier in their stomachs which prevents anything except digested food from getting by and so the indigestible parts of their meals have to come out the way they went in.

If one couples this with the charming habit most owls have of wolfing their prey whole there is a distinct possibility of re-creating the skeletons of the owl's food from the bird's pellets. Unfortunately there are some difficulties: the place the pellet is ejected may not be at all easy to find and only a minority of a particular owl's castings are likely to be available. However, detailed observations have enabled some research workers to build up a very clear

Tawny Owl showing toes beginning to spread and legs to straighten as it strikes a Wood Mouse.

TYPICAL OWL PELLET   TYPICAL SELECTION OF SMALL MAMMAL BONES   MATRIX I.E. UNDIGESTED FUR

A typical owl pellet and the jumble of bones and fur that it contains.

picture of exactly what an individual bird has been eating.

These studies have been carefully compared with the pellets ejected by owls in captivity. Here one can control exactly what the bird eats and find all the pellets it casts. These investigations have shown that some bone does get digested but seldom does a small mammal's or bird's skull not come back – once eaten. The pellets are damp and covered with mucous as they are ejected and it often takes the owl a minute or two to cough one up. Long bones (sometimes feathers and even the complete legs of waders) form the central core of the pellet and the rest of the material is usually embedded in fur. Pellets are often cast under a favourite perch and may accumulate in heaps if the site is sheltered. This is often the case when Barn Owls roost inside buildings. Otherwise the pellets cast in the open will quickly break down in wet weather.

The pellets vary in size, shape and structure according to the species of owl and may look rather different according to what the individual owl has been eating. Barn Owl pellets are generally very dark with a 'wet-look' varnish on them when reasonably fresh. Tawny Owl pellets are often pale grey and may look quite like a fox dropping – indeed many people have mistaken the two. Once you look inside, the differences are very obvious, for the bone fragments that pass through a fox will be thoroughly shattered and chewed but in the owl's pellet they will be largely undamaged. Little Owl pellets, and those from other small owls that eat lots of insects, are often bejewelled by shiny flecks of dark blue chitinous wing-cases from the large beetles they take.

The study of pellets can become an obsession and some analysts have looked at thousands, even tens of thousands, to build up an overall picture of what the birds eat at different times of the year and in different habitats. This can be done by careful searches of the casting places so that the pellets can be dated accurately. The importance of the various prey species can be assessed and the importance, to those species, of owl predation can also be measured. Such work is not to everyone's taste and most people probably think it rather a disgusting occupation. In fact, the owl's digestive activities clean up the remains very completely and the bones that you have to deal with are beautifully 'prepared' and not in the least bit 'dirty'.

The indigestible bits and pieces that make up the pellets also include remnants from other prey items as well and not just the bone and fur and feathers from small mammals and birds. For instance many species eat earthworms and the earth from inside the worms and the chaetae – the bristles on the outside of the worms' body used for gripping the side of the burrow – come back in the pellets. Whatever is inside the prey will come up, too – for instance earthworms may have contained vegetable matter and the small mammals may have been eating seeds.

Pellet analysis can be a very exacting scientific study. If all the clues to what

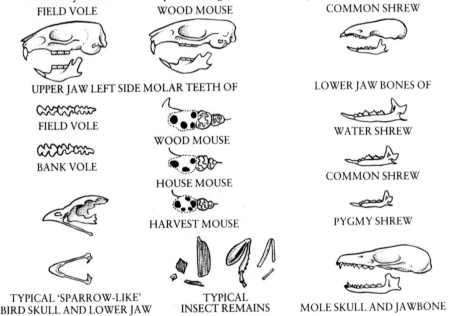

FIELD VOLE   WOOD MOUSE   COMMON SHREW

UPPER JAW LEFT SIDE MOLAR TEETH OF   LOWER JAW BONES OF

FIELD VOLE

BANK VOLE

WOOD MOUSE

HOUSE MOUSE

HARVEST MOUSE

WATER SHREW

COMMON SHREW

PYGMY SHREW

TYPICAL 'SPARROW-LIKE' BIRD SKULL AND LOWER JAW   TYPICAL INSECT REMAINS   MOLE SKULL AND JAWBONE

Identification of more common remains in owl pellets (from D. W. Yalden's Identification of Remains in Owl Pellets, *published by the Mammal Society, c/o Linnaean Society, Burlington House, Piccadilly, London W1; this booklet provides comprehensive information.*

the owl had been eating are followed up this will mean microscopic study of the small items in the pellet, for example, to see if there are earthworm jaws and chaetae in it. The former are much more useful; there was originally a pair of jaws for each worm, and their size will give clues as to the size of the worm. However it is possible to get a very great deal of information by collecting pellets and looking at the bones in them systematically at home, without a lot of scientific equipment. In Britain it is generally reasonably easy to work out which owl species was responsible for any pellet you find. Abroad the greater variety of local species in many areas make life much more difficult. In any case the best evidence is to see the bird at the roosting site or nest where you get the pellets.

The table below gives some information on the pellets of the common

THE PELLETS OF COMMON BRITISH OWLS

Species	Size (length x breadth)	Description & where to find them
Barn Owl	30-70 x 18-26mm Max 2·7″ x 1″	Dark, compact pellets, shiny when fresh, with smooth exterior. Often found in large heaps in buildings used for roosting or nesting.
Little Owl	20-40 x 10-20mm Max 1·5″ x 0·8″	Pale grey even when fresh. Not very solid, often with blue insect chitin. Found near or in nest or below roost tree.
Tawny Owl	30-70 x 18-26mm Max 2·7″ x 1″	Grey and felted when diet is small mammals. Easily found at or under nest or roost.
Long-eared Owl	20-60 x 14-27mm Max 2·3″ x 1″	Pale grey with harder surface and more digested fur than Tawny. Under nest or roost (particularly in winter).
Short-eared Owl	35-70 x 18-26mm Max 2·7″ x 1″	Dark grey but not shiny like Barn Owl's when fresh. Later paler. Near nest or at winter roost sites on ground.

British owls. If you are in Europe on holiday you may find the same species there as well as others, so there is a good chance of having a guess at what species the pellet has come from. Really detailed examination of pellets, using a binocular microscope for dissection, is getting more technical than most people would like. But one way of improving the quality of information you can obtain is to have a reference collection of feathers and fur so that you can compare what you find in pellets to identify those bits as well as the parts of insects. Most people are interested mainly in the identification of the vertebrate prey taken.

The real experts tend to weigh, measure and sketch each pellet before dissecting it, but this is rather pointless if you are simply looking to see what the birds have been eating. So the first thing to do is to tease the pellet apart to find out what remains are inside. Most people prefer to do this with the pellet dry but some think a slight dampening helps. Certainly a couple of mounted needles and a pair of fine forceps are really useful at this stage. If a small lens on a stand is available you can get a better look at small items like the earthworm's jaws or bits of beetle that might otherwise be missed. The furry and feathery material will generally be discarded unless the analyst is really keen and what remains will be more or less recognizable bones.

At first the only obvious bits may be smashed skulls and the distinctive lower jaws in a variety of sizes. The illustrations show how to tell the different species apart and this is quite easy, given a bit of experience and care. Do not be misled by your expectations of what your local small mammal population should be. Many a time owls have proved the mammal people wrong and have been eating species that were supposed not to occur locally. Some owls are really very good at producing pellets containing rarities like harvest mice and dormice. In the Tring area they also get hold of the bigger introduced edible dormouse *Glis glis*. Though identification is interesting in itself, even more interesting is to know how many animals are represented in the pellet. The easiest way to do this is to count either skulls and upper jaws or pairs of lower jaws after the identification of species has been made.

Quite apart from jaws, there will also be masses of other bones. Do not discard these. Some may obviously belong to birds – hollow long-bones (from legs and wings) or very obvious bird skulls and beaks. Others may prove a bit of a puzzle – owls may eat frogs and toads, fish, newts, lizards and even snakes. Experienced pellet delvers will take it as an affront to their expertise not to track down all such unusual bits and it is quite often possible to get help from local naturalists or the local museum. Once the identification has been made it is a very good idea to mount the identified remains on card, using glue, as you would do with dried flowers, so that they can be used for comparison with what may be found in the future.

There is a very good chance that a local bird club or naturalist's association would like to publish a short article about the results of such pellet analysis. After all, they are of interest to both bird and small mammal enthusiasts. For such a publication the time of year when the pellets were cast is important as is the species of owl and the habitat in which the pellets were found. Quantification of the number of animals eaten is also very useful, if you can establish it, and the diet of the owl may be expressed in several different ways (see page 53). It is very important, in any publication, to make clear exactly whether you are expressing diet as the number of animals or as total weight; they can give very different results. For instance, the average water vole at 100g (3½oz) is worth more than twenty pygmy shrews at 4g (0.14oz) each!

Bird identification, from bony remains, is very tricky; if you are lucky and the skulls and bills have come through then you can make a good guess. Otherwise your best bet is to collect road casualties and boil them up; if you can bear this, it will provide you with an identified reference collection of bones to compare with what comes out of the owl's pellets. Such ghoulish activities have failed to endear birders to generations of mothers and wives. It is not illegal, under the current protection laws, to do this provided that the bird bodies you use are road casualties or otherwise come by without breaking the law.

The owl's menu

A whole book could be written about the food of just the Barn Owl worldwide. Huge numbers of publications have appeared with details of many, many more Barn Owl meals than any reader has had hot dinners. This is because there is so much information available on their diet from looking into the cast pellets, which are so easy to find. In fact it would have been a very boring book as the answer to the general question of what owls eat is simply small mammals. This applies just as much to the largest as to the smallest owl but there are, as you will see, some exceptions and some variations.

Clearly there are the exotic, specialist species that are adapted for other prey. The amazing fishing owls (see page 12) are probably the most

Primeval wardrobes

One does not readily associate owls and wardrobes but there is a strong connection in the form of that irritating pest, the clothes moth. Have you ever wondered what the clothes moth did before there were humans who stored clothes in their houses, thus providing huge stores of food and ideal living conditions? The clothes moths are mostly from the group Tineidae, which includes several species whose larvae are found in the wild in disgorged owl pellets. These are ideal homes as they contain lots of fur, from the small mammals the owl had eaten, and the owl's digestion will not have even started to break down the keratin that the larvae eat.

Often pellet collectors will find that quite large numbers of moths, of several different species, will emerge from a cache of pellets that they have collected and put to one side. The moths will not have done any damage to the material within the pellet that most analysts want (the bones) and they may even find that the conversion of the fur to caterpillar droppings makes the task of separating it from the interesting bits easier.

IT'S AMAZING WHAT YOU SEE EMERGING FROM AN OWL PELLET....

interesting; these birds show clear adaptions for their own chosen way of life. Otherwise the main variations in food are between the smaller species, which tend to concentrate on insect prey – of which the British example is the Little Owl – and a variety of other species which are more or less adapted to take birds.

For example, anything small and furry is attractive to the Barn Owl and so any small terrestrial mammal that rustles in the grass had better watch out – shrews, mice, voles, rats, moles, dormice, squirrels, hamsters, susliks and even stoats and weasels have been found in Barn Owl pellets; most European bats have turned up too. Birds up to the size of thrushes are also often eaten – apparently usually when they are roosting; so sparrows, finches and starlings are particularly well represented, unlike other species which are not communal roosters. Frogs, toads, snakes, lizards and large insects are also on the menu – sometimes rather frequently in southern areas.

Detailed studies show that most (more than 90% by weight) of the diet consists of small furries; in some studies (Poland in autumn) up to 14.5% of the diet was of birds. Apart from small mammals, birds, frogs, toads and bats

... A BABY, YES, BUT IT'S UNTHINKABLE THAT AN EAGLE OWL COULD TACKLE AN ADULT WILD BOAR...

comprise the rest of what they eat. In Britain a massive study mostly during the 1960s, published by David Glue, indicated 97·7% terrestrial mammals, 2·1% birds and 0·2% others – mostly frogs and toads and a few bats. The studies, covering nine different areas in Europe and reported in the *Birds of the Western Palearctic*, were the result of the analysis of no fewer than 242,999 pellets – hot dinners three times a day for well over 200 years!

The most southerly European owl, Scops, is unusual in that it eats a lot of larger insects like grasshoppers, crickets, beetles, moths and dragonflies, also millipedes and worms. Though it does eat small birds, lizards, mice, bats and shrews, these are a very small part of the diet. Most other owls, from the Eagle to the Pygmy, relentlessly pursue small and furry creatures.

Of course for a bird the size of an Eagle Owl lunch does not have to be so small, and it is almost a case of if it moves the Eagle Owl will eat it. Mammals up to a hare in size are regularly taken as also are birds up to Mallard size. Most prey are relatively small but the literature records wild cat, wild boar (presumably a youngster) and young roe deer as well as cat, dog, lamb and calf. In some areas hedgehogs form a major part of the diet. Maximum and minimum proportions of various items of the diet from studies in Sweden, Germany, France, Spain and Morocco are as follows:

	maximum	*minimum*
Mammals (not rabbit, hare)	91·5*	7·7
Rabbit & hare	83·7	1·2*
Birds	59·5	6·1
Reptiles, amphibians & fish	2·8	0·1

* Morocco, where 73·2% of the diet was Jerboas!

The Little Owl is a species of very catholic taste with all sorts of foods featuring in different studies. It is difficult to quantify the different foods, for a variety of soft-bodied invertebrates may be eaten in profusion at certain times of the year and their remains don't turn up in pellets. Certainly invertebrates, including large and small insects (particularly beetles, cockroaches, craneflies and moths) as well as millipedes, woodlice and earthworms, feature on the menu whenever they are available. Small mammals, small birds, reptiles and amphibians are also included. Little Owls were accused of the 'crime' of taking many young game birds, but this was disproved many years ago. They have also been suspected of invading and decimating Storm Petrel colonies in parts of Wales.

The Tawny Owl tends to concentrate on mammals, though it also eats birds and amphibians. Out of ten European studies the maximum and minimum percentages recorded for different items were:

	maximum	*minimum*
Mammals	100*	50.4
Birds	46·6	1·8
Amphibians	14·3	0
Other (bats, lizards, fish)	4·0	0

* In Italy, this study omitted from further three categories.

In Britain the majority of studies confirm that small mammals make up the bulk of the diet by weight; then come slightly bigger species, like rats, rabbits, moles and water voles and finally birds (between 5 and 10%). The most vulnerable birds are again those that roost communally, which may be taken in dusk and dawn swoops. However, as one would expect with a woodland owl, individuals of non-gregarious species are also taken. The size of birds eaten can vary from Goldcrest to thrush size. Though frogs may be taken in large numbers at spawning time by particular owls, overall they are not very important. We don't really know how many worms they eat because pellets would have to be examined in great detail to find them; where detailed studies have been done they have shown a lot of earthworms.

The Long-eared Owl is again largely a small-mammal eater, with a regular leavening of a few birds and there are several records of bats being taken: very few of frogs.

In some studies the food of Short-eared Owls has been shown to be almost exclusively voles. Certainly they are mammal-eating birds; all five studies summarized in *Birds of the Western Palearctic* show that more than 90% of the diet, by weight, is fur and not feather. The British and Irish owls seem to eat the highest percentage of birds – generally moorland breeding species such as pipits, finches and buntings.

You would be right in thinking that owls concentrate on the same sorts of food in temperate areas. In Britain, for instance, one would be hard-pressed to defend any of our native species of owls against a charge of mammalocide. You would assume that the size of owl would make some difference to what size mammals it ate – if small mammals varied a lot. In fact 'small mammals' are mostly small – there is not much available in the countryside between voles and rabbits. The possibilities are therefore restricted and, in any case, from the owl's point of view, as often as not food is food if it rustles in the undergrowth – often the pouncing bird will have little idea exactly what it is about to kill and eat. Mostly it will be small and furry – that will do nicely.

Display

For most species of birds there are well known and obvious displays which have been described by ethologists, biologists who study behaviour, but there is a real problem with most owls: when they are awake and most active it is generally dark.

In fact much of the information that is conveyed by diurnal species through displays is exchanged between owls by voice. In the darkness of the breeding hole the young Tawny squeaks at its parents and siblings to indicate that he or she is owl and not food. An unwelcome visitor to the nest is subjected to a machine-gun barrage of emphatic bill-clicks. The parents have loud and eerie calls to advertise their territories rather than elaborate and colourful feathers and associated advertising displays.

However even the most nocturnal birds do see something of each other and most species have displays associated with pairing, the continued good relationship between the adults and the defence of the territory. The moth-like flights of the Barn Owls at dusk and dawn are used both for feeding and also as a very conspicuous advertisement of the bird's continued maintenance of the area as feeding territory. The exaggerated wingbeats at the start of the climbing circle of a displaying Short-eared Owl are but a prelude to the spectacular dive which is the culmination of an elaborate sexual 'come on'. And the familiar 'just a'sitting and a'lookin' behaviour of Little Owls on their nesting tree – often within a few feet of the entrance hole – is pretty good at warning off any intruders, their size or smaller.

One trait shared by many species is head-bobbing or circling when the birds are disturbed. At one time this was thought to be done for the effect it had on other owls and animals. It is now thought to be more to do with the owl's inability to judge distance and movement very well except within the usual hunting range. The slightly different viewpoint gives more perspective on the scene.

Most species try to melt into their surroundings when threatened but, if they realize that they have been spotted, they present as big a silhouette as possible to the intruder, often standing side on and dropping a wing for effect. The eared species tend to remain face on and raise the ears. Sometimes, if the threat is from below, the owl will lift its wings half up and make as if to stoop downwards – again maximizing its apparent size.

Unclean

Two of the main lists of birds in the Bible, Leviticus and Deuteronomy, are concerned with noting the varieties that were considered ritually unclean. These include owls. Ritual uncleanness has little or nothing to do with the amount of time the bird spends preening or washing but is to do with its life-style.

The species that are considered 'unclean' and an 'abomination' are mostly those that prey on other vertebrates and are therefore contaminated with the life-blood of other creatures. A few are on the list because of their carrion-eating habits and some may be there because of long association with pagan gods. However with the owls their reason is clearly that they prey on God's creatures and it therefore behoves God's people not to become contaminated by eating them.

There are several passages in the Bible where owls are associated with coming to a nasty end. For instance Isaiah's prophecy (34:13) of the end of Edom includes 'and it shall become a habitation of dragons and a court of owls' and goes on to mention screech owls and great owls taking the place over. Earlier Isaiah foresees that after the overthrow of Babylon the 'owls shall dwell there' and, in Zephania, that within the ruins of Nineveh 'the owl shall hoot in the window'. Clearly these associations are not just to do with the uncleanness of the owls but also with their predilection for rather desolate and scary places. As the Psalmist says (102:6-7), when feeling decidedly down in the dumps:

I am like a pelican in the wilderness,
I am like an owl in the desert.
I watch and am as a sparrow alone upon the house top.

The nest

No owl, certainly none of the British and European species, could be accused of being a skilled nest-builder. Most make no attempt to build a nest, but take over a hole, existing nest or other structure, or even a small tract of ground and simply scrape a suitably sized depression for the eggs to stay together. Most reports of proper nest-building have probably actually been owls taking over existing nests and just moving the old nest material upwards and to the edge of the old nest or, just possibly, because the bird that had originally built the nest was itself refurbishing the structure whilst the owl was also in possession.

The table of European owls and their nest sites (on p.59) shows that preferences are about half and half for holes and for open nests of some sort. The biggest holes used are probably the large, gloomy recesses preferred by the Barn Owl: barn roofs, the attics of disused farms and huge hollows in large trees (elm, oak and ash are those most often occupied). These are often traditional sites used year after year. In Britain the next size downwards is the snugger accommodation chosen by Tawny Owls. Often this is down the broken-off and hollow branch of a large tree but the inside of an old squirrel's drey or Magpie's nest will do. Some even nest in rabbit burrows or

A Little Owl brings food, an earthworm, for its chicks at a nest in an old rabbit burrow.

"IT'S MY HOLE"

holes in the root system of a tree and a very few nest on the ground under vegetation. Our smallest owl, the Little, chooses such small holes it sometimes has quite a squeeze to get in. In some parts of Europe Little, Tengmalm's and Pygmy may regularly take over woodpecker holes from the very large Black Woodpecker – unknown as a wild bird in Britain.

The other tree-nesting owls generally choose the old nests of other birds. In Britain 80% of Long-eared Owls breed in old nests of crows and about three-quarters of these are in conifers. The two big European *Strix* commandeer particularly the old nests of Goshawk and Buzzard; Urals are very happy with nest-boxes, whereas Great Greys very seldom breed in enclosed surroundings. In the northern forests Hawk and Great Grey Owls are fond of nesting on the top of a broken-off stump of a good-sized tree. The other species are ground-nesters with the main requirement for a Snowy Owl being a patch that clears of snow early in the spring. Short-eared Owls generally nest on a bank with a good cover of heather or tussocky grass to

OWL NEST SITES

Species	Sites preferred	Height above ground
Barn Owl	Hole in building, tree, cliff or quarry. Nest-boxes.	Tree sites 2-9m (7-30ft)
Scops Owl	Hole in tree or man-made structure. Nest-boxes.	Up to 10m (33ft)
Eagle Owl	Ground, cliff or old nest in tree.	0-60m (0-200ft)
Snowy Owl	On ground on hummock or outcrop.	0
Hawk Owl	Top of stump, old open nest, hole in tree. Nest-boxes.	Up to 13m (40ft)
Pygmy Owl	Hole in tree (woodpecker). Nest-boxes.	3-8m (10-28ft)
Little Owl	Hole in tree, cliff, building, even the ground. Nest-boxes.	0-12m (0-40ft)
Tawny Owl	Hole in tree, old enclosed nest. Nest-boxes.	0-25m, ave. 10m (0-80ft, ave. 30ft)
Ural Owl	Hole in tree, open old nest, stump, even ground. Nest-boxes.	3-16m, ave. 10m (10-52ft, ave. 33ft)
Great Grey Owl	Old nests of large raptors. Stumps. Even ground or cliff.	0-20m, (0-70ft)
Long-eared Owl	Old open nest – mostly crows. Some on ground.	Ave. 7m (23ft)
Short-eared Owl	On the ground.	0
Tengmalm's Owl	Tree holes (inc. woodpeckers). Nest-boxes.	2-8m, ave. 6m (6-25ft, ave. 19ft)

conceal the nest. Eagle Owls may be in the open, often on steep ground, but most nests are sheltered in some way and many are on cliffs or banks – often quite high up.

Owls are obviously quite set in their ways when it comes to the choice of a home. However, within the clear limits their genetic make-up imposes on them, they are still able to exploit their changing environment. For instance Barn Owls have not been able to exploit man's buildings for more than a few thousand generations: a very short time in the life of a species whose ancestors were certainly around 10 million years ago. However a man-made cavity is, logically, no different from a natural one in a cliff or tree; owl nests have even been found in abandoned cars, quarry machinery, etc. An interesting change has come about recently with the Ural Owl in Finland. As more and more areas of forest are being managed for timber production the

Leaving its nest site, also used as a winter roost,
a Barn Owl begins hunting in the fading light.

number of stumps and rotten trees (their traditional nesting sites) has decreased dramatically (they have been removed for fear of infection spreading to the other trees). As this has happened the Ural Owls in the north have been forced to occupy the previous year's open nests of Goshawk and Buzzard. In the southern part of the country owl-lovers have provided them with nest-boxes which have been readily occupied.

As we shall see (page 89) many owls are not very tolerant of their own kind. However there have been cases where they have proved to be successful neighbours with other birds of prey. For instance Edmund Fellowes found a nest in a barn in Buckinghamshire during 1967 which had both Barn Owl and Kestrel incubating within four feet of each other. The nests shared the same entrance and both were successful, with five young Kestrels and three young Barn Owls fledging. There are even some Little Owls that breed in the enlarged tunnels of Sand Martin nests on the periphery of active colonies. Although they do cause disturbance, and more than once the owls have been seen making rather clumsy attempts to catch the martins, the two species seem generally to co-exist without too much 'bovver'.

Nest-boxes

Almost all hole-nesting birds can be enticed to nest in boxes of a suitable design; owls are no exception and even those that do not take to holes can be persuaded to nest in artificial structures or prepared sites if you are lucky. The best results come from knowing your local owl population: there are definitely fashions in the sort of site used which vary from place to place. Try to discover what is the local fashion in nests, and make your nest-box mimic it; for instance, if the local Tawnies nest in holes in tree trunks, make your boxes with large holes.

There is good evidence that birds take rather little notice of the outside of a nest site and that the important thing is the shape and size of both the cavity and the actual hole itself. Security is an important consideration – if a box is too low, often disturbed by people or has your cat regularly sunning itself on its top, then the chances of getting an owl to use it are not good. Because owls tend to be territorial throughout the year, there is little chance of getting an owl immediately to occupy a newly erected nest unless local sites are in terribly short supply. It seems likely that Tawny Owls, for instance, have often made up their minds as to which site they will nest in by October of the previous year. This means that it is well worth putting up owl boxes at any time of the year since the longer they are up the more chance they have of being selected.

Owl boxes are fairly large structures and become much, much heavier the further one has to carry them. It is a good idea to make sure that they will last as it can be tedious having to replace flimsy ones every few years – just when they have weathered nicely and the owls have accepted them. There is no real alternative to wood as a construction material but to make a range of boxes from newly bought sawn and planed wood could cost a fortune. Happily the birds are probably more at home with old, rough-hewn planking than superb new timber. Old floorboards from a demolition site are ideal, planks from old pallets, off-cut sawn timber from the local saw-mill, old packing cases and even ammunition boxes can all be cheap and suitable. The designs can and should be modified to take account of the material you have available.

With the designs intended for erection in trees you should always think of the health of the tree and future generations of humans. Do not use heavy-duty nails or screws in wood where there is *any chance* of someone using a chainsaw – awful injuries can be caused. From the tree's viewpoint remember that it is still growing (unless it is dead) and the box will be pushed

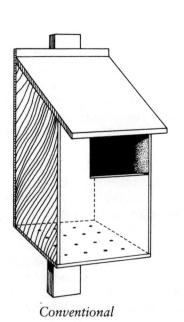

Conventional

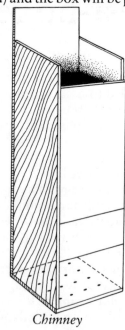

Chimney

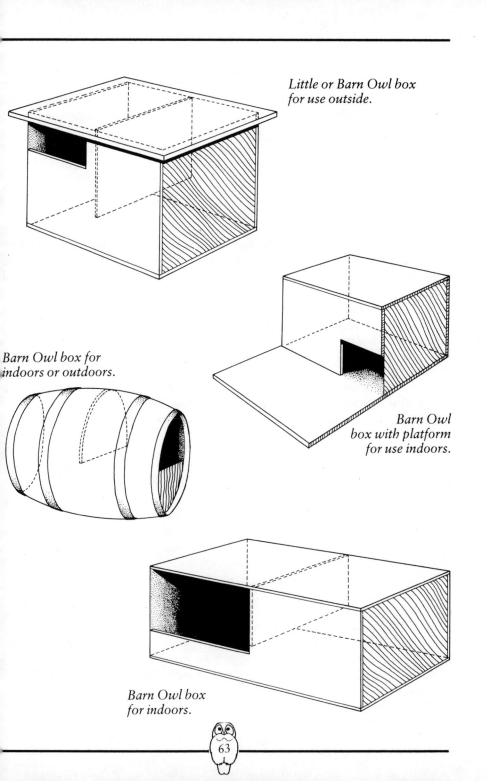

*Little or Barn Owl box
for use outside.*

*Barn Owl box for
indoors or outdoors.*

*Barn Owl
box with platform
for use indoors.*

*Barn Owl box
for indoors.*

off the trunk or branch as the tree grows round the nails or screws. In the best of worlds brass screws, undone every year by a turn or two to allow for the tree growth, are ideal. Failing that, hardwood dowelling or copper nails are absolutely safe alternatives from the chainsaw safety angle. Tying the box on using plastic baler twine or wire is acceptable but the ties must be loosened regularly or eventually the tree or branch will be strangled and die.

Box design

The two classic owl designs for tree-nesting species are: one that mimics a hole in a tree trunk – like an ordinary Blue Tit box but rather larger – and one that simulates a hollow branch. The latter is particularly useful for Tawny Owls and may be almost irresistible to them in some areas where there are mature trees which are 'looked after' so that there are few, if any, natural holes.

Where tiny owls breed, in Europe, conventional nest-boxes measuring 15cm (6in) square and twice that height may be used but, in Britain, a Little Owl box should be 20cm (8in) square (or in diameter) and some 50cm (20in) high at least. Chimney boxes (see illustration on previous page) can be twice this height as Little Owls seem to like to be in a really dark place when they nest. It may even be worth making a box with an inner entrance (see illustration) to attract them since, in many areas where they nest, there are often many suitable holes and the box has to be very attractive to be successful.

Tawny Owl boxes should have entrances 15-20cm (6-8in) square with boxes measuring at least 25cm (10in) square and 80cm (32in) deep. Chimneys of up to 150cm (60in) can be used if there is enough material. It is not important that the nest chamber should be dark for this species. In many wooded areas high holes are preferred and a ladder may be needed to get at the best sites. In secluded areas low boxes may be used – some Tawnies even nest in rabbit holes underground. A few regularly use open nests – usually old ones made by corvids (crow family).

Barn Owls are rather a special case since the most likely nest-boxes to be used are actually sited inside buildings. Here one of the most important considerations is to make sure that it is safe from farm cats. You must also, obviously, ensure the owls always have access to the building. All sorts of box may be improvised – a barrel with half one end taken out and used as an internal baffle. An old wooden orange box – with a central partition – fixed in the apex of a barn used to be ideal but oranges do not come in that sort of box any more.

For Long-eared Owls several people have been successful in attracting birds to nest in 'artificial' old corvid nests. These are woven from willow and firmly attached at a reasonable height in a good looking conifer. The bare bones of the woven nest are seeded with an inverted turf in which the owls (or other raptors) can scrape the nest hollow.

The most enormous nest-boxes are needed for the big *Strix* like Ural Owls. A standard nest-box would measure 120cm (48in) high and 60cm (24in) square. Made from substantial planking to ensure that they last a good time, these are very unwieldly things to carry round the forest. One ardent owl fiend in Finland stacked the replacement boxes for his extensive study area in his garden – 64 boxes neatly piled 2 high and 4 deep were the size and shape of a moderately sized room – 8 foot high and wide by 16 foot long.

All sorts of elaborate means of recording what goes on in a nest-box have been rigged up. One can simply position a hide nearby and watch what happens. The wide availability of video equipment now makes it possible to have a remote camera set up and monitor what is going on from a distance – or watch later on videotape. One stage further is to have the inside of the box bugged for sound and either to record this or have it played in the hide. For special studies an automatic camera which operates every time a bird breaks a light beam at the entrance can be used. Although it is possible to use 35mm equipment with large magazines the easiest kind to use is cine equipment on single frame used in conjunction with electronic flash. These studies can produce such good shots that the prey brought in can be identified and even have its weight estimated. Rather surprisingly owls quickly get used to the necessary lighting.

However it is usual simply to climb up to the box, open it up and look in. This is not always safe – either for the bird or the observer. Barn Owls at a nest site are likely to be pretty nervous of intruders doing something strange in the immediate vicinity of the nest – whereas they will happily carry on if it is simply the farmer going about his ordinary tasks. So visits to record the nest contents should be carefully spaced and, in any case, licensed by the Nature Conservancy Council, as the Barn Owl is on Schedule 1 of the Wildlife and Countryside Act. Nest recorders and ringers for the British Trust for Ornithology can get this through the BTO; otherwise applications should be made to the Nature Conservancy Council (NCC), Northminster House, Peterborough.

The danger of Tawny Owls deserting their nests if disturbed is in the early part of the breeding cycle – during incubation and a few days after the young have hatched. After that there is little danger of the birds being disturbed by visits. However there is a very real chance that the owl parents will attack intruders at or near the nest and the possibility of this should always be borne in mind – Eric Hosking, Britain's premier bird photographer, lost an eye to a female Tawny. Any defensive attack is likely to come from behind an intruder and will be totally silent. It is a good idea to have a friend on watch and if you do find a female who attacks, take precautions – such as wearing a fencing mask. I have seen a ringer, at a nest in a broken-off cherry tree, clanged four times by a female who had earlier knocked the person who found the nest out of the tree.

Probably the best advice is always to be careful. If you approach the box without trying to conceal the normal noise you would make walking through the woodland and then tap the box gently with a long stick before trying to look in you will have warned the bird and, in most cases, she will leave of her own accord. If you look in and the female is still there – leave her alone and, next time you want to make a visit, make even more noise on your way to the box and when you get there. This lessens the risk of desertion.

Conventional
The basic construction of this type of box is simple. The provision of a one-piece roof overlapping the sides is a good idea. If sufficiently wide timber is available it is an advantage to have the grain vertical but, for particularly big boxes, a framework with small planks nailed sideways across the frame may be needed. Decent sized drainage holes are needed at the bottom; for a Little Owl especially, some fibrous peat should be placed in the box to stop light from coming in.

Erection on a slightly over-vertical trunk is best done with a batten keeping the body of the box off the tree. It is always best to check the tree carefully for areas of green lichen or other indications of wetness – these should be avoided.

Chimney
These are best made from wide planking with overlapping sides (see illustration on p. 62). The entrance can be straight down the open end or in a side – in which case this should be the lowest edge when the box is erected. An inspection and cleaning hatch needs to be constructed near the bottom but not at it. If it is right at the bottom the contents of the nest might roll out after debris and other material have accumulated. The box should be erected in any position where a large branch may have rotted, at the usual heights at which the prospective bird nests (see p. 59). A batten or ties should be used to fix it firmly.

With this style of box an added refinement is to include a mirror so placed that a torch can be shone at the mirror, its light reflected down the box and the contents seen in the mirror. This is quite tricky to fix up but well worth the effort if it means that you do not have to take a ladder out with you every time you want to check it out.

Little special

Because Little Owls seem to be rather shy of nesting in boxes to which the light gains admittance a baffled box, like the one illustrated, may be advantageous. The entrance area may be used by the birds to roost in whilst they decide whether to use the inner sanctum for nesting. Both this and the nesting area may be used for pellet casting – nest-boxes often provide good numbers of pellets for analysis. For this species boxes erected in pollarded willows along a hedge or stream may be particularly favoured, again, at the normal nesting height (c. 3m/10ft).

Barn Owl

Most are to be erected within buildings where there is unrestricted access for the birds and can therefore be made of less durable materials. The provision of an inner area, well sheltered, is necessary for the actual nesting attempt but it is also a very good idea to have some area available for the young to flap their wings and see a little of the world go by as they develop. To be really successful nests outside buildings have to be weatherproof and pretty big. Typical natural nest sites are down at ground level within the hollow trunk of a really big old tree.

Artificial nest

These are woven from willow twigs and should be securely wired together. It may even be a good idea to incorporate a layer of wire netting to ensure sturdy and lasting construction. Only experience can teach you where to put it and that will only come after you have either found or been shown a good number of natural Long-eared Owl nests. The embellishment of the nest with a sod is very important as this will make it look and feel like an old, used nest of a crow or other species. Even if no Long-eared Owl uses it, you can reckon you have been successful if any of the diurnal birds of prey takes it over.

Sex and the single owl

The first problem faced by an owl which wants to breed is to find a mate of the same species – and to make sure that the bird which it sets out to woo is of the opposite sex. The latter may seem a real problem to the bird-watcher, who can generally see no difference at all between a male and a female owl of the same species. Clearly it is no problem for a Snowy Owl; even humans are able easily to recognize the plumage differences between the sexes (see p. 17).

So what do the other species do? Quite simply they rely on behaviour and on voice to make sure that they are not wasting their time. First of all the voices of the different species are distinct and ensure that a Little does not become attracted to a Tawny – or vice versa. Secondly the territorial calls (see p. 20), are, for most species, much more likely to be given by the males and so the females can seek them out and choose who to woo. When the pair has become established there will usually be a fairly long period during which they are able to get used to each other and defend their territory together. At this stage other owls of the same species seeking a territory will be able to tell not only that the area is occupied but also that there is a potential breeding pair in residence.

It is clearly very important that the birds of a breeding pair should become properly acquainted with each other and the relationship shouldn't suffer 'irretrievable breakdown'. Owls are endowed with powerful weapons and the last thing that should happen between a breeding pair is for aggression to break out, for either could easily severely damage, possibly even kill, the other. As part of their courtship, males and females of species that fly in the day have elaborate aerial displays and it is likely that the nocturnal species also indulge in such flights – but in the dark. The birds often sit together and preen each other (technically called 'allopreening') – a very strong mutual indication of trust. As the breeding season approaches the pair often look at potential nest sites together although, for a number of species which have been studied in detail, it seems to be the female that makes the final choice.

As the time for egg-laying approaches (and this varies a lot according to species, see p. 70), the male will catch food and pass it to the female. This ritual, known as 'courtship feeding', could and probably does serve several purposes. First of all it helps the female build up her reserves and produce the necessary material for making the eggs she will be laying. Secondly it reinforces the bond between the two birds. Finally it will give the female an indication of how well her mate will perform when it comes to providing her with food during incubation and for the brood after it hatches. At the same time it may well help her to decide, though almost certainly not consciously, how good the food supply is for the coming breeding season and thus to regulate the number of eggs she will lay. For several species it is clear that the female will not even start to lay until the male is catching and presenting her with more food than she is able to eat.

Copulation is a fairly simple process. Birds of both sexes have a single uro-genital orifice below the tail: the cloaca. This gets its name from the *Cloaca maxima* which was the main sewer of Ancient Rome! In copulation the male jumps on the back of the female who twists her tail round and downwards whilst the male twists his upwards and around in the opposite direction. The cloacas meet and sperm is ejected from the male's penis, situated on the wall of his cloaca and everted in copulation, on and into the female's. The process may take a rather shorter time than you have spent reading this description. During the period shortly before laying and whilst the clutch is being laid copulation takes place regularly – sometimes several times in the space of an hour. Quite often the arrival of the male with an item of food is the signal for another bout (the owl equivalent of an invitation out to dinner). The important copulation that fertilizes the eggs takes place only hours before each egg is laid (blunt end first).

Since the owl pair is, by now, firmly established and the two birds are quite at ease with each other, they have not developed the elaborate pre-copulatory displays seen in other groups of birds. With many species, particularly

.... AGAIN ?!

where the breeding pair only comes together just as the breeding season starts, very complicated behavioural systems sometimes apply. This is taken to extreme lengths with the lekking species, where the female chooses a male on a special display ground only at the time when she is receptive and the male has nothing to do with her either before or after fertilization. In comparison the owls are rather dull, stay-at-home species with pairs remaining together, year after year, defending the same territory and nesting in one or other of two or three preferred sites within the territory. For most pairs divorce will be unlikely but re-marriage will quickly follow a bereavement.

Breeding seasons

It is not realistic to set out exact breeding seasons for the different species of owl since the timing, even within Britain, will vary from year to year and also depend on both height above sea level and latitude. A cold spring may put the season back by four or more weeks and certainly the most northerly Tawny Owls will lay eggs up to six weeks later than their southern cousins. Birds breeding in sea-level woods in Northumberland will be at least a fortnight earlier than upland ones only a short distance away.

For lowland birds in southern England the approximate dates, for a normal year, for first egg-laying would be as follows:

Tawny Owl	*March or early April*
Little Owl	*End of April*
Barn Owl	*April*
Long-eared Owl	*March*
Short-eared Owl	*End of March or April*

Of the British owls only the Barn and Short-eared are known to have second clutches and so, with them, the season may continue through much of the spring and summer. This will only happen where the vole populations are high. For the other species even replacement clutches where the first has been lost at egg stage are rather infrequent. Sometimes a number of very early clutches may be laid by both Tawny and Long-eared in February. If the weather then deteriorates these may be abandoned and the same birds may lay replacement clutches when the weather improves.

Owl eggs

All owls lay plain white eggs which are rather rounder than those of most other birds. Their chalky whiteness, contrasting strongly with the marvellously marked and camouflaged eggs of so many other species, is a sure indication that the owls have descended from ancestors that nested in secure holes. In a hole the colour of the egg is not at all important in concealing it from a predator, for if one has got into the hole the eggs will surely be eaten. Rather it is important for the eggs to be very pale, white is best, for the parents to see them and gather them together during incubation.

The fact that even the owls which now nest in open nests on the ground or in trees still have white eggs might seem a puzzle because in these situations camouflage would protect the eggs. The reason cannot be that this is a recent habit, since there is good fossil evidence that species of some of the open-nesting owls have been around for millions of years. However, the parent owls almost always start incubating their eggs as soon as the first has been laid and so they are not normally going to be exposed to the view of a potential predator. All species are nocturnal and, during change-overs, when there is hardly any light, the whiteness of the eggs must be helpful – even in the open-nesting species.

The size of the eggs varies with the size of the species that lay them. The smallest European owl egg is the Pygmy Owl's and the largest is the Eagle Owl's. Some comparative measurements are given in the table overleaf. Of these species, owls of the genus *Strix*, like the Tawny in Britain, have particularly round eggs and Long-eared and Snowy rather more ovoid ones. This is clear when one looks at the ratio of length to breadth in the table.

TABLE OF OWL EGG SIZES

Species	Female wing length (mm/in)	Egg dimensions length (mm/in)	width (mm/in)	weight (gm/oz)
Barn Owl	290/11·4	40/1·6	32/1·3	21/0·7
Scops Owl	161/ 6·3	31/1·2	27/1·1	13/0·5
Eagle Owl	482/19·0	60/2·4	50/2·0	73/2·6
Snowy Owl	448/17·6	57/2·2	45/1·8	59/2·1
Hawk Owl	238/ 9·4	40/1·6	32/1·3	21/0·7
Pygmy Owl	105/ 4·1	29/1·1	23/0·9	8/0·3
Little Owl	166/ 6·5	36/1·4	30/1·2	16/0·6
Tawny Owl	278/10·9	47/1·9	39/1·5	40/1·4
Ural Owl	363/14·3	50/2·0	42/1·7	46/1·6
Great Grey Owl	452/17·8	53/2·1	43/1·7	50/1·8*
Long-eared Owl	299/11·8	40/1·4	32/1·3	22/0·8
Short-eared Owl	319/12·6	40/1·6	31/1·2	21/0·7
Tengmalm's Owl	176/ 6·9	33/1·3	26/1·0	13/0·5

* Estimated. Other measurements are the bare bones of much more detailed information available in *The Birds of the Western Palearctic* (see bibliography). The wing length here refers to the flattened and straightened measurement of the longest wing feathers from the bend of the wing.

All species may occasionally lay deformed eggs. These are generally much smaller than usual and may not contain a yolk – it is thought that they are often laid by young birds. Some may be laid with a double yolk, but it is believed to be impossible for twins to hatch from such an egg as one or other of the chicks would run out of food before reaching a viable size and being able to hatch.

The kleptomaniac hobby of egg collecting was all the rage in Victorian times, and earlier this century. Nowadays all owl eggs are fully protected under the Wildlife and Countryside Act. Eggs have been very important in the studies of the effects of pesticides on wild examples of diurnal birds of prey and Heron species. Thinning of the eggshells, following sub-lethal effects on the calcium metabolism of the adults, has been a worrying symptom in some species. Results show that although there are toxic chemical effects on owls this does not seem to lead to eggshell thinning in the same way as suffered by other species.

Just a'sittin' and a'waitin'

The incubation period must be the most boring time for the female owl. She spends all her time sitting and waiting, keeping the eggs warm by contact with her naked body, where she has lost the feathers of her underparts. This 'brood patch' develops at the start of the breeding season and the veins under the skin become enlarged to act as efficient exchangers of heat with the eggs. This engorgement of the veins is stimulated by the contact of the naked skin with the smooth shell of the eggs.

The table (see p. 76) shows that the incubation periods for owls range from three and a half to five weeks and, for the whole of this time, it is the female that does the sitting. Not that the male is a complete chauvinist; he will feed his mate as well as himself. Even if a liberated male owl suddenly decided to help incubate he would not make too good a job of it for it is only the females that develop brood patches. The female only ever leaves the nest for a very few short bouts of exercise and to defecate. Just for these short periods the male, of open-nesting species, will take over sitting on the eggs – despite his lack of a proper brood patch. In some studies these absences have amounted to just over 10 minutes a day. This is real devotion to duty: the continuance of the species.

For all the species studied in detail the chicks have been heard to start calling within the egg hours, sometimes more than a day, before they hatch. This is probably very important indeed, for the little chick, when it does hatch, is not unlike one of the small mammals the birds eat. It would be truly tragic to treat one's first-born as food. In some cases, for instance with Barn Owls, the female has been watched during the hatching process and has gently and carefully helped her new chick from the shell – certainly not something that all birds do.

THEY'RE DEMANDING FREEDOM OF SPEECH, EQUAL OPPORTUNITIES AND A FIVE DAY WEEK....

Of course this is not the end of the long spell of sitting and waiting since the young chicks need to be brooded, again virtually continuously, whilst they are unable to control their temperature. This takes a few days in warmer areas, but up to a fortnight after hatching for open-nesting species in the Arctic. There is also the problem of the later laid eggs which may carry on hatching for a week or two. The female Snowy Owl, in years of plenty of small mammals (resulting in large broods), might therefore be tied to the nest for seven or eight weeks. Life must be very boring indeed to start with although, when the young have hatched, there are domestic duties to perform like tearing up the prey brought by the male and feeding it to the family. The hen bird is also responsible for keeping the nest clean.

How many eggs to lay?

Most owls feed on small mammals and, notoriously, small mammal populations go through times of great abundance and times of real scarcity; even in southern Britain small mammal populations exhibit this cycle, in the Arctic it is even more marked and for some species, like lemmings, it is very regular with a period of about four years. The female owl then has a problem when it comes to egg laying; should she lay a large clutch or a small one? If the former, will there be enough food to feed them later on? If the latter, will she have lost an opportunity to raise more young?

Owls do not consciously work out the odds but the result of the behaviour patterns which have developed through the ages maximizes the chance of getting it right – in the end. First of all the female is able to assess, from her own hunting results and from the activities of the male in bringing food to her, what the position is at the time of laying. Then most of the females start to lay their clutch, with an interval of a day or two (or three or four) between

each egg. Females of species that specialize in small mammals start to incubate their eggs immediately. This means that the young hatch at regular intervals and are nicely graduated in size in the nest. If the food supply falters or fails the weaker, younger, chicks die from starvation (and get recycled by the starving parents or siblings). Nature red in tooth and claw, but very economical.

Species	Average clutch size (bad-good year)	Egg laying (interval/days)	Incubation (period/days)
Barn Owl	4 – 7	2 or 3	30 – 31
Scops Owl	4 – 5	1 – 3	24 – 25
Eagle Owl	2 – 4	2 – 4	34 – 36
Snowy Owl	3 – 9	ca. 2	30 – 33
Hawk Owl	4 – 9	2	25 – 30
Pygmy Owl*	4 – 7	1 – 2	28 – 30
Little Owl*	2 – 5	1	27 – 28
Tawny Owl	2 – 5	3 – 4	28 – 30
Ural Owl	2 – 4	1 – 3	27 – 34
Great Grey Owl	3 – 6	2 – 4	28 – 30
Long-eared Owl	3 – 5	2	25 – 30
Short-eared Owl	4 – 8	1 – 2	24 – 29
Tengmalm's Owl	3 – 7	2	25 – 32

* Incubation starts towards or at end of the laying period for these species.

The three European species that mainly feed on insects and other invertebrates are the only ones that do not habitually start to incubate the first or second egg, but wait until the entire clutch is laid. In detailed studies it has been shown that the first egg takes a little longer to hatch than the last and so the hatching interval may generally be just a little shorter than the laying interval. This is probably a good thing for some birds. One Great Grey with a large clutch produced its last egg 12 days after the penultimate one!

Growing up

The hatching of the eggs is the turning point for the nesting attempt. The tiny chicks which emerge are quite unable to do anything for themselves except to take the morsels of food offered them by the female and, most important, to call reassuringly to her to make certain that she knows who they are. The graduated sizes of the chicks in the brood are generally very obvious but there is seldom overt aggression between the youngsters. In times of food shortage the smallest one (or ones) may die but they are unlikely to be killed by their parents or siblings until moribund.

*Long-eared parent bringing wood mouse prey for its chicks
at an open nest in the usual conifer site.*

The eldest gets the best treatment, for the female owl will brood all her youngsters until the youngest is able to cope without her body heat. At this stage the first hatched may be quite a strapping young owl. Species which are fed on insects and other small food items can pick them up and feed themselves within a week or ten days of hatching. Species feeding on small mammals may not be able to handle food for themselves until they are a month old or even more.

Baby Tawnies already outside their nest in a hollow trunk, though still a long way from fledging.

It is characteristic of young owls of many species that they leave the nest well before they are capable of free and confident flight. Indeed many species are still fluffy lumps when they start to clamber around the branches of the trees. If they fall down they are able to hook themselves up the tree again using strong claws and beak and using the stumpy wings for balance alone. Clearly the young are vulnerable at this stage to being eaten by foxes or badgers or, in the trees, by corvids or birds of prey (even other owls are a great danger). The parents are good at defending the brood and the youngsters are fairly good at concealing themselves. In some species the unfledged brood may wander hundreds of metres – up to half a mile – from the nest.

Preparation for flight carries on all through this period with enthusiastic wing flapping and, eventually, inexpert short excursions. Free flight is not the end of their dependence on their parents. The youngsters have to be able to fly well and know how to hunt before they are independent. This can take a few weeks from fledging – as in the Barn Owl – or may be delayed for months in a similar sized species like the Tawny Owl.

STATISTICS FOR YOUNG OWLS

Species	Age of brooding (by hen days)	Nest departure (days)	Good flying (achieved)	Independence (weeks)
Barn Owl	ca. 10	50 – 55	Very soon	10 – 13
Scops Owl	2 – 3 (if warm)	21 – 29	Immediate	7 – 10
Eagle Owl	ca. 14	40 – 50	10 days later	25 – 30
Snowy Owl	Up to 14	14 – 28	4 weeks later	15 – 17
Hawk Owl	8 – 10	30 – 34	A week later	ca. 15
Pygmy Owl	10	30 – 34	Immediately	8 – 9
Little Owl	7	30 – 35	A week later	8 – 9
Tawny Owl	10 – 18	25 – 30	10 days later	15 – 17
Ural Owl	7 – 10	ca. 25	1 or 2 weeks	14 – 16
Great Grey Owl	14	20 – 28	5 weeks later	18 – 22
Long-eared Owl	7	21 – 24	10 days later	12 or 13
Short-eared Owl	6 or 7	ca. 20	2 weeks later	9 – 11
Tengmalm's Owl	15 or more	28 – 36	Soon after	9 – 11

NB. All timings are given from hatching date.

Just a squeak in the night

One of the least endearing habits of the Tawny Owl is the persistent squeaking of the newly fledged youngsters for food. This has variously been described as a 'rhythmical and monotonous series of squeaks' and 'an infernal racket'. Basically it is all to do with the parental strategy of devoting a long period, after fledging, to ensuring that the young get a good start in life.

Since the birds are out of the nest and the parents may arrive back with food at any time, all the young squeak, 'Mum, Dad, I'm here, give it me', in the hope that they and not their equally greedy siblings get the food. It can interrupt sleep for humans as the owls are at their most vociferous when it's dark (say 10 pm to 3 am in mid-summer) and much invective and many a bedroom slipper has been hurled at them. The only good thing is that they will eventually stop, after about 10 weeks or three months, sometime in late July or August when the parents kick them out of their natal territory. Until then, if you are blessed by a family of owls in your garden, ear-plugs are a practical suggestion!

Owls on the move

In Britain one does not normally think of owls as being migrants. After all the Tawny and Little Owls of the countryside are there throughout the year and clearly do not move much, if at all. However Barn Owls are sometimes seen

Migrant Long-eared flying in from the sea.

far from their usual breeding areas and so obviously this species can be mobile. Any bird-watchers who visit the East Coast during autumn can also see real owl migration when Short-eared and particularly Long-eared Owls come across the sea from Scandinavia in the autumn – their northern breeding areas get much too snowy for them to be able to stay the winter out.

On the Continent the Scops Owl is a true summer migrant and actually winters south of the Sahara. This is probably because many of the largest insects, its main food, are in fairly short supply, even in southern Europe, during the winter. Rather few Scops manage to stay in Europe all the year through and then only in the southern part of their range. The rest move southwards in late autumn (September and October) and can be found in their southern winter quarters, south to the Guinea Coast in the west and to Kenya in the east from October through to March. Some of these small owls probably have a round trip of 15,000 km (9,000 miles) from their breeding grounds in the vicinity of Lake Baikal, USSR, to Africa and back again.

For other species the patterns of migration may vary greatly from one part of the species' range in Europe to another. For instance southern breeding birds may be able to remain on their breeding territories throughout the year whilst the severe winter weather, further north, drives those breeding birds southwards or westwards to warmer wintering areas. This is the case with both the eared owls (*Asio* species): many northern birds move a thousand or more kilometres. However for many of the woodland species there is little movement, even of the northern birds, for it is always possible for them to find some food in the shelter of the trees. Probably, for these birds, it is extremely important that they should keep their breeding territory from year to year, when the hard-won knowledge of the small mammal's habits and habitats can be utilized again and again.

Migration is not the only sort of movement that the owls make. Initially even the sedentary species disperse away from the territory where they were hatched and reared and take up residence in a new area. This may take place a few weeks after fledging, for young Barn Owls, and they then may settle for life within 50 km (30 miles) of the original nest. In Britain 3 out of every 5 young Barn Owls were found within 10 km (6 miles) of the natal nest but in Holland they move further with 2 out of 3 within 50 km (30 miles). Barn Owls may move several hundred kilometres: the current record is 1,650 km – more than 1,000 miles. For a stay-at-home species like the Tawny Owl such distant dispersal from the breeding area is most unusual and most British chicks settle to breed within 10 or 20 km (6 to 12 miles) of their original nest. Continental birds may move a bit further but the record is of a Lappland Tawny which went 745 km (460 miles).

Finally there are irregular movements of owls which are their response to the cyclic pattern of abundance of their prey – particularly voles. In years when voles are scarce in an area both the adult and young owls will be forced to move much further than in other years. Under such pressure the owls of several different species may be found far from their normal areas and even such high Arctic species as the Snowy Owl may come southwards into temperate areas. In Europe Hawk and Tengmalm's Owls are particularly well known for this sort of movement (often termed 'irruptive'); this turns into truly nomadic behaviour if the birds then settle to breed far from their original sites.

The northern Long-eared Owls are fully migratory and move south and west to winter in areas where they find a good food supply. In southern parts of the range there may be rather little movement and the species is seldom found to the south of the southern limit of breeding. The autumn passage period is quite late not starting until the end of September and lasting into late November or even December. Movements are very variable from year to year and Britain may receive rather few birds in winters when vole populations in Scandinavia are high. Returning migrants reach the East Coast in March, April and May. Our own birds are certainly not such dedicated migrants but the ringing returns do show that they are more mobile than Tawny Owls.

The Short-eared is another highly mobile owl. Migrants from all areas of Europe move southwards and westwards and it is probably only the

Two Dunlin, potential meals, panicked by a Short-eared quartering a saltmarsh.

southernmost populations that contain truly sedentary elements. Some birds cross the Sahara to winter in Sahel areas just to the south of the desert. The extent of the movements undertaken depend crucially on the state of play with the voles in the areas the birds reach. Good numbers will cause them to break their journey and, as likely as not, to stay to breed in the area during the next summer. This means that very high densities of breeding birds may build up with the vole numbers and birds from all over the place may congregate to breed at one area in one year and far away in the next. Such movements of breeding concentrations depend on food supply and therefore vary from year to year. There are plenty of ringing recoveries from other countries to match the British bird who was found in Vologda (USSR)!

Nomads

Nomadic humans follow their herds of goats and flocks of sheep from one seasonal pasture to another, pitching their yerts or laying the bedrolls where they find the grass. When we talk about nomadism in owls we are looking at a similar behaviour but one not performed quite so neatly or regularly. Human nomads tend to be moving from lowland winter to upland summer

pastures, possibly diverting for the early grass in a sheltered valley on the way up. Nomad owls are following the populations of small mammals, not as the individual animals move but as their numbers in the different areas ebb and flow. In Arctic tundra there may be a hundred times as many small furry dinners running around one year as there are in the next (or even from one month to the next); clearly the potential for owls to live and breed is much influenced by such fluctuations.

Owls will therefore often breed cheek by jowl in areas where voles are present in large numbers but have to move on to find where the voles have peaked in the next year. Ringing recoveries show that such species as Short-eared may move to breed thousands of kilometres from where they were themselves reared. Detailed census work shows that territories, in the same place, may be more than a hundred times bigger in poor vole seasons than in the best.

Town owl, country owl

Human beings have made a huge difference to the world. We tend to think of town and country as very different sorts of places – the majority of us now rather more at home in the former, and the majority of birds, mammals and other wildlife more at home in the latter. This is probably to delude ourselves. Certainly in Britain there can be very few areas with owls which have not been drastically modified by human activities and whilst some parts of the country may mimic 'natural' habitats fairly closely almost all our owls exist by exploiting habitats created by man.

For instance, the vast majority of our Short-eared Owls, at first sight denizens of the untouched wilderness, are to be found breeding in either moorland areas or young forestry plantations. Human influence on the latter is very obvious and, within a few years, the trees get too big for that species to be able to exploit the area. They are well able to take the hint and move on to a more favourable area as, in any case, they are adapted to a nomadic life-style (due to fluctuations in prey). However, with a few notable exceptions, like the flow country (natural wet peatlands) of the northern part of the mainland of Scotland, our bleak moorland areas are the product of man's destruction of natural forests over the last few centuries.

Where food is available and there are suitable breeding sites, you will find owls. In Britain the most likely species in an urban area is undoubtedly the

Tawny. Some take to eating many more small birds, like sparrows, than their country cousins; others do very well on rats and mice which, themselves, are attracted by human activities. In the London area there are many good-sized trees with suitable breeding holes in the parks and even in some of the squares and larger gardens. Roughly half the inner London area, mainly the western part, was found to have Tawny Owls during the detailed breeding atlas work of 1968-72. More recently the London Wildlife Trust 'Owl Prowl' did a good job in increasing the Londoner's awareness of owls and found the Tawny to be even more widely distributed than before.

Whilst none of the other owls have taken to a fully urban life-style, Barn, Little and Long-eared can occasionally be found in town areas. Long-eareds are generally much more likely to appear in winter when roosting birds may take up residence in suitable scrubby areas. Barn Owl numbers have gone down so much in recent years that there is very little chance of finding truly urban pairs now – there would have been a few decades ago. The Little Owl can become a town resident, but only in the more spacious suburbs. For instance none was found breeding in the 24 inner London tetrads (2km x 2km squares of the National Grid) but there were good populations in Richmond Park and near the Lea Valley gravel pits and reservoirs.

It's all Greek

The scientific name of the Little Owl is Athene noctua. *'Athene' because the Greeks, in ancient times, thought the Goddess of Wisdom, Pallas Athene, appeared to them as an owl. The human shape of the Little Owl and its penetrating yellow eyes probably led to this myth. The Goddess Athene gave her name to the City State of Athens, and the symbol of the owl (readily identifiable as the Little Owl) appears on the early coins of the city.*

Roosting

To a normal bird roosting means where it spends the night. In the topsy-turvy world of the owl it is, of course, a question of where it spends the day. Owls can have their lives made a total misery if they are spotted by little birds during the day for they will be unmercifully mobbed (see p. 99).

Short-eared Owls at a communal roost.

Many of the hole-nesting species will roost in cavities, where they are available, and thus be concealed from the other birds' prying eyes. In particular Barn Owls are very likely to use traditional nesting sites for roosting throughout the year. However, holes are not always available, particularly for the woodland species, and many Tawnies, as well as open-nesting birds like the Long-eared, roost in trees. They will generally simply perch on a branch, upright and quite close to the trunk, and keep motionless. This seems to work pretty well and Long-eared can sometimes be found in fair numbers in a favoured mature thorn thicket. Tawny Owls, except soon after fledging, will never be found in more than twos: the adults of the local territory. The birds of a pair may be fairly close together and can even be found concealed in the evergreen fronds of ivy enveloping the trunk of the same old tree or building.

The Short-eared Owl also regularly roosts communally. However it tends to choose a sheltered site under a grassy bank in sand dunes or moorland.

The Snowy Owl does not deign to conceal itself but often seeks shelter, against the worst of the wind and weather, in a tangle of rocks whilst still making sure that it has a good view. It can often be spotted, with the naked eye, at long range, where the underlying colour of the rock is a dark grey. The pale plumage is a dead giveaway.

In the Mediterranean the Scops Owls exploit their superbly adapted intricate plumage pattern to appear like short, broken branches. They are so sure of the efficiency of their camouflage that birdwatchers may spot one, raise the binoculars and then decide that it is, after all, just a branch. If they venture too close the branch will actually fly away.

Finding roosting owls, during daylight, has two advantages. First it is the only good opportunity one has to study the plumage in detail on the live bird – short of becoming a bird ringer and catching them or cheating in a zoo. Secondly the roosting site is often the place where the pellets are coughed up and so searching roosting sites is likely to reveal a treasure trove of evidence of the food preference of the birds.

Territoriality

For most species of owl territory is of over-riding importance. This is their bit of ground. They must feed, hunt, nest, roost, preen, lay their eggs, raise their young and teach them how to fend for themselves on this precious tract of what, to us, may seem unprepossessing real estate. The species that stay in the same place may get to know it very well indeed over a lifespan of ten or more years. Even the other species, which may have to move on after a year when vole numbers crash, will get to know their patch exceptionally well. After all, their lives depend on it.

The territorial imperative has led owls to develop the beautiful haunting calls that advertise their presence and ownership to each other. This civilized way of behaving, far short of the dangerous clash of heads favoured by many ungulates, only works because the implications behind the call are understood by all. The call means that the bird is in possession, it knows the area, it will almost certainly be able to repel any attempt at dispossession because of its local knowledge – and it will do so. It is therefore not in the best interests of a potential rival to make a direct challenge.

New territories tend to be carved out by newcomers at the intersections of three or more existing defended areas. A small patch may, at first, be all the

upstart is able to steal – just a minute amount of ground from each of three or more neighbours; almost as important, he will begin to get his voice recognized as 'local' by them. Once that has happened, provided that the food supply is reasonable, he should have it made and will eventually carve out sufficient ground to support a family. The newcomer will, of course, be in an excellent position to take advantage of any mishap that befalls any one of three neighbours.

Internecine strife

It has long been realized that owls and other birds of prey sometimes kill each other. Their remains have been found amongst the prey at nests as well as in pellets. However the importance of this behaviour was not fully realized until Heimo Mikkola, a Finnish owl expert, took the trouble to bring together all the information scattered both in the literature and also in the Finnish bird archives. The picture that emerged was not a pretty one. Within Europe several species of owl are quite likely to attack and kill other, smaller owls nesting near them!

The size differences between owls are enormous, so the smaller species could not attack the larger ones. However, the degree of aggression shown does not just reflect the bird's body size. True, Heimo Mikkola found that the largest, the Eagle Owl, was by far the most aggressive; it ate all the 12 other European owls as well as 18 different species of daytime birds of prey. There are even records of full-grown Eagle Owls being eaten by others of the same species. The list of Eagle Owl victims discovered by Mikkola is very impressive; he found the remains of almost 1,300 owls and over 700 daytime birds of prey which had bitten the dust. The owls that Mikkola studied had eaten a large number of other predatory birds, of which twice as many were other owls as were daytime birds of prey. Of the victims most (a third) were Long-eared, followed by Buzzards, Tawny Owls, Kestrels and Goshawks in that order.

Ural and Tawny Owls are also quite aggressive, though not on anything like the scale of the Eagle Owl; Urals seem to prefer Tengmalm's and Tawny to prefer Little Owls. Goshawks were the commonest killer of owls amongst the daytime birds of prey: they took more than three-quarters of the victims that Heimo Mikkola was able to trace. Again the unfortunate Long-eared was the most frequent victim with Tawny and Short-eared as runners-up.

Several species seem to be very tolerant of other raptors and owls in their territory, with very few victims recorded. Great Grey, Snowy, Hawk, and Long- and Short-eared are certainly equipped to take the smaller species and yet don't seem to do so. The smaller species of owl are, of course, at a grave disadvantage in a fight; Mikkola couldn't find any taken by Scops or Pygmy Owls.

These patterns of aggression can be partly explained by the life-styles of the species concerned: first of all it is obvious that many owls and birds of prey will be directly competing for the same prey. It therefore makes sense for the strongest ones to 'take out' their competitors. However there are several species that would appear to be in a dominant position and able to kill other species, but which do not attack them. All of the potential killers are breeding in parts of their range where they are likely to encounter others, so it is not lack of opportunity. However these owls are also 'nomadic' which means they tend to move to areas where the small mammal populations have peaked. If they get it right they have no need to kill any competitior – food will be abundant. Indeed any bird showing acute aggression would probably run more risk of injury from its aggression than it would gain by reducing the competition. Hence so little aggression in the massive Snowy Owl which is nomadic, as compared with the huge Eagle Owl, which is much more sedentary.

On the Continent these considerations have real conservation implications. The Eagle Owl is now protected in many areas where it used to be shot for sport and so the breeding population is expanding. However each breeding pair has a large territory and some (not all) of the resident Eagle Owls will systematically remove competitors from it. These include other owl and raptor species which may, themselves, now be rarer and more worthy of our protection than the Eagle Owls themselves. In Britain it is clearly prudent not to put nest-boxes for both Little and Tawny Owls up on the same tree or even very close to each other.

How many owls?

It is not easy to count birds; for a start, what are the terms of reference? With small birds, the population of residents will be twice as high at the end of the breeding season as at the beginning – after winter mortality has taken its toll. Then which year are you talking about? If the species is affected by cold weather the population after a run of bad winters may be only 10-20% of what it would be after a mild decade. Should the figure include migrants? The British residents of many species are joined by large numbers of migrants from the Continent for the winter.

So, for owls, let's set some reasonable limits. First of all the figure should apply to the British and Irish breeding populations and will represent adult pairs that should be holding territory at the start of a breeding season. None is very severely affected by cold winters but the figures are given for a normal run of years. Where winter migrants swell the numbers these are in addition. Such overall population figures give rather little idea of what the maximum local density of birds might be so this, again measured in territorial pairs, is an extra statistic worth investigating.

The figures have been taken from sensible guesses using the best information currently available. There have not been countrywide surveys of owl populations involving bird-watchers counting every owl over the whole country. There have, however, been what are called 'national atlas surveys' in which every 10km square of the National Grid has been surveyed. These have been organized by the British Trust for Ornithology (in conjunction with the Irish Wildbird Conservancy) for both breeding birds (1968 – 72) and wintering ones (1981/82 – 1983/84). These give excellent data on the distribution of the birds and estimates can then be made of the overall breeding population using density information from special surveys and from the Common Birds Census, also run by the BTO.

Of the owls the Tawny is the most populous, even though it does not breed in Ireland. It was recorded during the breeding bird atlas in 2,305 of the 10km squares – that is 60% overall. Clearly the density of breeding pairs within the country varies tremendously and fenland was completely devoid of them – no decent trees or woods. However in some parts of the country it must be difficult, if not impossible, to get out of hoot-shot of this species. The best estimate of breeding numbers is roughly 75,000 pairs. In the best woodland areas territories may be less than 10 ha (25 acres) over quite large areas. More typically, in wooded farmland, there may be three per 100 ha (roughly 80 acres each). These are much smaller territories than on the Continent where there are often many other species of owls competing with the Tawny, and so they are spread thinner on the ground.

Our second commonest owl, at the moment, is almost certainly the Little, even though it is really confined to England and Wales, having spread from introductions made in the middle of the last century. At that time the Tawny Owls (and other native owls) were having a pretty hard time from gamekeepers and most were on the decline. The real increase in Little Owl populations took place in the first thirty years of this century and could, possibly, be correlated with the steep decline in keepering associated with the First World War. Current estimates are that the British population is roughly 10,000 breeding pairs. They were found in 1,381 10km squares during the breeding atlas but were probably much more common within their range than the more widespread Barn Owl. In Britain and on the Continent three pairs per 100 ha (80-acre territories) would be a maximum density.

Although never so common as the Tawny Owl, Barn Owls would probably have been found in more 10km squares had the breeding atlas been run a century ago. The long-term decline in numbers certainly means that there are now fewer Barn Owls in Britain than at any time for which bird records exist. The atlas map shows them to be more widespread than Tawnies but with many white squares amongs the red: Barn Owls were found in only 2,279 (59%) of the squares compared with the Tawny at 2,305. However Barn Owls have much bigger territories and so the population estimate is well below 10,000 pairs and probably as low as 5,000. In areas where there are good numbers still left the territories may be as little as 400 ha (1,000 acres) each (even so, huge compared with the other species) and there are few extensive surveys where the average was not at

*Little Owl: note how the shaded pupil is
bigger than the one in the light.*

least five times this size. Just a few migrants from the Continent reach us
during the winter but they are so few that their presence will not make a
significant contribution to the winter numbers.

The second species of woodland owl, Long-eared, is exceptionally
difficult to find and count. It does appear in Ireland and, although it was not
found to be at all common during the breeding atlas field-work over most of
England and Wales, there were records from 942 10km squares in all. The
breeding population estimate is 3,000 pairs. British territories are probably
50 ha (125 acres) or so at their smallest although, in other parts of Europe,
these owls may breed very densely when the small mammal populations are

at a very high level. In some years several thousand individuals will reach Great Britain and Ireland for the winter from across the North Sea but, in a normal year, these may not number more than a few hundred. Many of the migrants roost communally in suitable thickets even in southern England and form a notable spectacle for birders.

The rarest of the regular British owls is the Short-eared – paradoxically one of the most conspicuous and easiest to see. During the breeding atlas field-work it was found in 802 10km squares (only one in Ireland where it has only nested twice). The areas it frequents are upland or coastal and the bird is a familiar sight flying over the ground in search of food during the day as well as at dusk and dawn. Breeding density is very dependent on the amount of prey and in a poor year the British population probably dips below 1,000 pairs; in a good one, it may be as much as three times this and even overtake its cousin the Long-eared. In good conditions territories can be down to less than 20 ha (50 acres) but they are seldom as dense as this and ten times this size might be more typical. Winter migrants and irruptive birds may swell the resident numbers by several thousand in a good winter when, if it follows a peak breeding year with good survival, there might be 30,000 individuals of this owl in Britain and Ireland.

That concludes the list of real British owls with the exception of the Snowy. In the only recent years when breeding took place there was but the single pair. In all there may have been 15 to 20 individual birds around in the country but now the figure is certainly less than 10 and breeding has not been possible because of the lack of a male for many years. Other migrant owls only reach us in single figures and then very infrequently – Tengmalm's could possibly break into double figures in years of peak emigration from Scandinavia but Scops are not even annual visitors.

Owl count

If you want to find out how many owls of the different species there are in your locality, why not try a personal survey? The idea is simple but the practical aspects can be a bit daunting. What you need to do is to plot, on a map, where each owl territory is by going out and listening for their calls and, if you are lucky, watching to see them.

The first step is to choose a sensible area. Clearly it gets a bit pointless to try to find out how many owls there are if the answer is *none* so it is as well to choose a patch where you know there are at least some! Once you have decided on a general area, fix the boundaries exactly and buy the Ordnance Survey 1:25,000 map of the area (they used to be called 'two and a half inch'). Try to avoid areas where there will be a lot of noise through the night – 24-hour industrial sites or major motorways are impossible. Make sure that there are roads or other rights of way that enable you to get around the area well and that there are no suitable owl sites more than a quarter of a mile (say 400 metres) from these routes you will use. Make tracings of the outline of the area and use one of these for each visit.

On each visit (ideally once a fortnight) record all the encounters you have with owls both as locations on the map and in your notebook. Give each visit a reference letter and copy the information onto master sheets – one for each species of owl. If you can manage it you may find it best to make the master sheets rather bigger in scale (say four times the size) as you may have a lot of information to copy on. Territorial calling of our owls peaks in February and March and the survey period should include these months but can also go on into the breeding season, for the recording of youngsters calling will give proper proof of breeding.

Recording should include descriptions of the owl calls as there are different noises produced by the same species to mean different things (see page 20). Do not worry if you are not sure, to start with, what the calls mean – or even what species makes them – as you will learn a great deal whilst surveying.

The most crucial aspect of recording is to try to work out which birds are calling at the same time and are therefore different individuals. This is the information which you will analyse to discover how many birds are involved. At the end of the season you should find that your master map, for each species, will have clusters of records indicating occupied territories.

Any results that you get will be much more interesting if you carry on and do it again in years to come; your local bird recorder will be interested in the results. (Contact can be made through the British Trust for Ornithology, Beech Grove, Tring, Hertfordshire HP23 5NR). If you have your own tape-recorder you may want to try to tape the calls from the different birds to see if you can recognize individuals – both within the same year and from year to year. Of course you will also come across other birds at night – if you are lucky, species like Nightjar, Nightingale and Woodcock may be found in heath or woodland. Other birds may fly over making very strange noises – near water they may be the flight advertising calls of Moorhens! During the spring migration period you may hear moving waders passing over. You may also come across nocturnal mammals – fox, badger and bats.

Map analysis

This example is rather simple but shows the hypothetical results for Tawny Owl in wooded farmland over five visits: A to E. The lines joining the same letters indicate simultaneous calls. There is no evidence that the owls heard in the two top woods are from different pairs but there is good evidence that woods 3 and 4 are occupied by different pairs and by birds different from those in woods 1 and 2. The answer, in this case, would be three territories.

Of course life is seldom as simple as this and, since both birds in the pair may call, owl analysis can be much more tricky than for songbirds where only the male sings. Quite soon, after you have tried it, you will begin to understand what is happening and realize the difference between the relatively relaxed and low-key calling between the pair and the assertive and aggressive sounds when a territorial boundary is at stake.

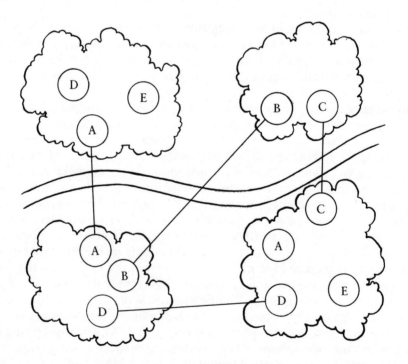

This sort of survey can be done on foot but a bike is excellent transport. For the former an area three miles (5km) in diameter round your home would be ideal; for the latter, five or six miles' diameter would be possible. If you try to cover a big area, for instance a third of a 10km square, a car may be essential (also if it is any distance from home). You will find it best to move a little way from the car to listen as, soon after it has stopped, the car will sizzle, cough and splutter. Distant birds may best be heard by cupping your hands behind your ears and should be recorded on your map by an arrow, indicating the direction from which the call was coming.

Birds can be provoked into responding to a tape call played at them. This is *not* recommended as good ornithological practice since the calls from your tape-recorder may make the owls think that there is an interloper about. Smaller owls, not of the species whose recording you have played, may shut up out of fear and could even be driven away if you kept on playing. Birds of the same species, not yet fully established in territory, may be put off. If you are going to try playing your tapes then you should:

1   Never use it straight away, always stop and listen for a few minutes for the birds to call by themselves.
2   Never play it very loud at first at any place.
3   Stop it as soon as you get a close response.
4   Only use it occasionally at any one place.
5   Do not use loud playback near houses; the owners might not appreciate it.

Finally it is as well to remember that your actions as an owl counter may look very suspicious to other people. You may even have the law called in to investigate you. It is just as well to have some identification on you and to be able to explain what you are doing. If you live in Buckinghamshire it might not be a good idea to choose to survey the area round Chequers when the Prime Minister is in residence and is entertaining the President of the USA!

Beware

From time to time, in Britain, there are reports of owls terrorizing neighbourhoods. Most often this turns out to be the blood-curdling calls and terrifying shrieks of the birds, causing those of nervous disposition to feel that the local ghouls, zombies, werewolves or even Beastie Boys fans are out to get them. Just occasionally there is good reason for their apprehension, since some Tawny Owls have been known to attack human passers-by close to a nest. Attacks at the nest are quite frequent, as owl-ringers and owl-nest-recorders can testify. Such people are aware of the possibility and take precautions but the ordinary man in the street who happens to be close to a hole in a tree that houses an aggressive female Tawny, cannot be expected to wear a fencing mask just in case.

In fact such attacks are much less common now than they were twenty years ago. This is probably because of better public awareness, even legislation, which means that far fewer young owls are now picked up and looked after by inexpert bird lovers. Such birds, returned to fend for themselves, can often be partly imprinted on man and may have lost that healthy fear of humans that would normally keep them well out of range. An owl that has become a real friend of its keeper should *never* be released into the wild for this reason.

Owls breeding in wilderness areas far from human habitation are also potential attackers. In particular the Eagle Owls of the northern forest, so large they have no reason to fear anything they normally encounter, may defend their nest or chicks against humans. One Finnish birder, walking through the forest, approached a trestle railway bridge late one spring. He stopped to listen for any approaching train before crossing it to avoid getting wet in the river. Next moment he was hit a violent blow from behind and was sent tumbling over the edge and down the scree. An Eagle Owl was nesting under the bridge approach and did not like him being there.

The Eagle Owl had chicks and most of the reported Tawny attacks come late in the breeding season when there are young in the nest. This is because the parental investment in the brood increases as the young reach fledging age. It therefore becomes more and more important to the parents that nothing happens to harm them and their behaviour becomes more and more daring in the defence of the nest and its precious contents. Of course the parent birds are not consciously working all this out; over the millions of generations of birds, those whose determination to look after their chicks has increased over the time they are in the nest have been most successful. Thus a gradual change in behaviour during the breeding season has evolved naturally in many different species of animals. (This change in parental behaviour can be observed also in humans.)

Mobbing

There seems to be nothing so provocative to ordinary songbirds as a roosting owl discovered in daylight. They flock together apparently taunting the unfortunate bird which often, to the human observer, looks totally bemused and even embarrassed by the whole process. The end result is generally that the owl is forced to move from its roosting place and, chased by the mobbing birds, will end up some way away. For the small birds doing the mobbing, which may themselves be territorial, this should reduce their chance of becoming a meal for that particular owl: there is safety in numbers when so many gang up together.

The mobbing does also, of course, make the potential predator conspicuous and therefore mess up any chance there is of it killing whilst the mobbing birds are making a noise. Often they have a specific alarm which will mean to others, of the same or different species, 'Hi there, chaps, owl alert, come over and help me out.' A Tawny Owl in woodland may attract more than 30 or 40 individuals of ten or a dozen species. Bird-watchers get to know these calls too and a roosting owl, already discovered by the local bird populace, may become the focus of the bird-watcher's attention too. Owls roosting in thick cover or holes in trees or buildings escape this attention. Human hunters know all about mobbing behaviour and captive, stuffed and even plastic owls have been and are used to lure other species within gun-shot range or even on to limed sticks. The latter has been illegal in Britain for many years but the sticks are still in use in some parts of the world. Beside the captive or stuffed owl lots of small perches, covered with sticky bird lime, form the ideal vantage points for the mobbing birds but those that choose them are stuck and caught.

Owls are also very useful indeed for luring down corvids. Hundreds of thousands, even millions, of Jays, Magpies, Carrion and Hooded Crows, Jackdaws and even Ravens have been shot in Europe over decoy owls. Nowadays the would-be decoy man can even buy a plastic inflatable owl! If he is not too good a shot and waits for the quarry to come close to the decoy a puncture repair outfit might be a good idea too. Trappers of hawks used also to use owls as lures in a special form of trap – a loose lump of wide mesh netting was set above the head of a captive owl set out in the open on a hawk migration route. Many of the passing hawks and falcons could not resist a swoop at the owl – straight into the net.

A Long-eared discovered at roost in dense hawthorn scrub suffers a tirade of abuse from (clockwise) *Wren, Greenfinch, Chaffinch and Blue Tit.*

Toxic chemicals

Over the last few decades mankind has been able to develop a formidable arsenal of death-dealing chemicals for use in the countryside. These include pesticides which directly kill pest animals – insects, nematodes, bacteria, etc. – and herbicides which are aimed at vegetation. Some of the most effective ones which were initially discovered and used proved to have disastrous effects on many animals at which they were not aimed.

In particular the chlorinated hydrocarbons introduced shortly after the Second World War – including DDT, Dieldrin, Aldrin, Gamma BHC and so on – proved to be persistent and damaging to top predators in the environment. Their effect was to build up in a number of sub-lethal doses through the food chain to become apparent, both as killing agents and also through sub-lethal effects, in such predators as the birds of prey and owls who were at the top of the chain in the terrestrial environment and Herons and grebes in fresh-water habitats.

The owls in Britain undoubtedly suffered. However, they include several species which are likely to be in the same bit of woodland all their lives and therefore, even at second remove, were unlikely to come across too much contaminated food. The species most at risk, and the one which declined at the time the chemicals were in use, was the Barn Owl. It often feeds in open agricultural habitats where chemicals are very likely to have been used. It feeds on small mammals that may accumulate sub-lethal doses in their bodies and has a very good chance of concentrating the toxins. There is good evidence linking the use of these agro-chemicals with the initial decline of this species. At the same time Little Owl numbers have probably declined in some areas and this too may be due to toxic chemicals.

However whilst such species as the Sparrowhawk and Peregrine are making a welcome comeback with the decrease of such chemicals, the Barn Owl is not. This may be because of pesticides of a different sort – that is, rodenticides of the anti-coagulant family (including Warfarin). The case remains, in many people's eyes, unproven, but detailed new research has been instituted to try to find out if there are any direct links.

Longevity

Birds are not noted for their longevity in the wild, for there are too many hazards. They may starve, be afflicted by some disease or parasite, fall prey to a predator (whose name is, as like as not, Tibbles), be hit by a car, crash into a window, fly into wires, etc. This is not the case with zoo birds or other captive specimens which lead a cossetted life of luxury with every meal carefully prepared and delivered to the beak. Such captive birds regularly live to twenty or more years with no problem.

In the wild the only evidence of age comes from ringed birds. The oldest wild owl on record was a Long-eared which lasted for over 27 years from ringing to finding. This was not a British bird, and the records from our own ringings are just under 17 years for a Tawny, over 13 for a Barn (both from samples of more than 1,000 ringed birds which have been found later) but 9·7, 9·1 and 6·7 years for Long-eared, Little and Short-eared respectively. One of the chicks from the Fetlar Snowy Owl's nest was found dead almost 15 years later – this was clearly a lucky individual. Large birds generally last longer than small ones.

Parasites and disease

This rather unpleasant section has to do with some of the facts of owl life and owl death that seldom make themselves known to the watchers. It is no real surprise to discover that such unpleasantness does afflict them for it is bad enough for us humans and the owls do not have a National Owl Health to call upon.

Since they prey on other birds, they are quite likely to catch external parasites, like fleas, feather-lice and louse flies (hippoboscids), from other species. Luckily, for the owl, these are often host specific and will not last long: certainly any mammal fleas will quickly look for a 'proper' host. There are a number of special owl-variety feather-lice which crawl around them and, quite regularly, their nests have fleas in them. The nests may even have beetles feeding on the fleas and other insects that specialize in eating the discarded bits of flesh and bone that accumulate there.

Internally all sorts of nasty things can happen to an owl ranging from malarial infections or TB, to various worms and other internal parasites. Aspergillosis, a fungal infection, may invade their lungs and they are susceptible to pneumonia. One very unpleasant protozoan parasite affects owls and other birds of prey feeding on infected pigeons. The parasites multiply in the oesophagus and trachea forming a cheese-like deposit known as 'frounce' by falconers – at its worst this may choke the bird to death.

Any form of disease which impairs the ability of the bird to fend for itself can be fatal. It is therefore rather surprising that quite large numbers of owls seem to be able to function with moderate parasite loads without dying. On the other hand the owls and the parasites will have evolved together and it is probably not a very good idea for a parasite to kill its host – and its free meal ticket.

Accidents

Like all of us, owls are mortal and their lives end in all sorts of ways. Unlike humans in the modern era and in a developed society, few die of old age and the majority die in circumstances where the verdict would be 'accidental death' – once they have survived the vital period in the nest.

Surviving to fledge – and then to become independent of one's parents – in the crucial first month or two of life is very much a question of luck. To be laid, as an egg, by an experienced female, mated to an experienced male, in a year when the small mammal population is high is the best start in life. It is very important that the young mammals should not be peaking when you are laid as the population may have crashed by the time you are out of the egg and your parents may have a really uphill struggle trying to provide food for the growing family. In such circumstances, if you are unlucky and come from a late egg in a large clutch, you may find yourself a terminal case, and just a factor in the growth of your older siblings.

Such a demise might correctly be described as an accident of birth. The developed young bird making its first foraging flights and beginning to fend for itself is exceptionally vulnerable. The period of parental guidance is very important as this clearly helps the young birds considerably for there is not the over-riding need to find food for survival. The family keeps together and ringing recoveries show, for most of the British species, that it is when parental oversight ceases that the maximum likelihood of tragedy striking occurs.

Often the food supply is still good but hunting performance may be in the learner or 'just passed the test' league rather than emulating the Fangio, Stewart or Mansell prowess of the adult birds. Knowledge of the local area is still being built up and collisions with objects like wires, poles, branches and even tree-trunks cause casualties and eventual death. Young birds concentrating on a mouse or vole beside a road or railway may be wiped out by a speeding car or train.

Before they were afforded protection this was also the stage, from August through September, when many birds were shot or trapped by keepers intent on minimizing the losses at Pheasant rearing pens. Anything with a hooked beak was the enemy and shot-gun, trap and poison would be used against owls as well as other birds of prey. This is becoming much less common as the protection laws are respected, the number of old-style keepers dwindles and many people come to realize that a pretty effective way of managing your Pheasant rearing regime is to minimize the losses from all sorts of predators rather than attempt to attack the killers directly.

Whilst the risk of such accidents is highest with naive young birds it does not disappear completely even for older and wiser birds. Traffic accidents and collisions with wires continue to take their toll. As the breeding season approaches there are risks to be taken in searching for nest sites: this is the time of year when birds are reported inside buildings or trapped in crevices – obviously prospecting for nesting sites. It is also when the chances of being murdered by another owl are at their highest.

Rather surprisingly drowning appears to be the cause of death for significant numbers of owls. These accidents often take place in artificial containers – water-butts, cattle troughs, etc. It may be that the birds get thirsty and come down to drink and then get trapped. Alternatively it is just possible that the sound of lapping water may trick them into thinking there is a small mammal scurrying about and they strike at it – splash down and then can't get out.

In the vicinity of larger areas of water one of the unkindest accidents happens to both young and old birds – entanglement in fishing line. The tough monofil line used by fishermen is easily strong enough to entrap a flying owl and where a cast has become tangled in branches a deadly trap may be set for the next patrolling owl. A part of the familiar local air-space, until recently safe and recognized, becomes an unseen and deadly trap. Often a wing, or just the wingtip, becomes entangled and the struggles of the owl to free itself only serve to bind it more strongly to the deadly line. In Britain this peculiarly unpleasant death is regularly visited upon Tawny Owls beside lakes, reservoirs and rivers.

Changing fortunes

Bird ringing in Britain started almost eighty years ago. An analysis over this period of the different recovery methods (basically, causes of death) for the three most common species of owls is very instructive. The percentage of shot and hunted birds was highest for Little Owl but, for all species, dropped markedly with the introduction of protection in 1954. Railway casualties have remained static, as a proportion of all recovered birds, throughout the period. The amount of railway traffic and its speed has not changed much. However road casualties for all three species have increased greatly to reach 30% or more nowadays. Indeed the Barn Owl has the unfortunate distinction of providing a higher proportion of road deaths, amongst dead ringing recoveries of the species, than any other bird in Britain. Road traffic has increased greatly in both volume and speed not only since the start of ringing but even over the last couple of decades.

First aid

The first thing to do, when you find or are given any injured bird, is to put it somewhere quiet, dark and reasonably warm for a period of two or three hours. This is often all the treatment a stunned bird needs and it will be fit for release none the worse for its KO. If the bird is wet and dirty, a clean-up and dry is essential before it can be put away in the ubiquitous cardboard box for recuperation. A Little Owl found floundering in one of our local canals needed 20 minutes' work with the hairdryer (absorbent towels or tissues do just as well).

If there are more than superficial contusions or the bird has obvious broken bones or cannot flap properly to be able to fly it should go to an expert for care. If you do not know anyone, try your local RSPCA, birders or even the police. Birds that seem to be in one piece may be suffering from starvation and only need a couple of days of intensive feeding to be well enough for release. The best food would, of course, be rats or mice but day-old chicks (get them from your local hatchery) will do very well. I have even heard of a Tawny thriving on dogfood; if you do use it, make sure it is a good meaty one and does not contain lots of cereal. It should be wrapped up in the hairs of the cat or dog to give the owl some roughage. This is not enough for young birds

BARRING UNFORESEEN ACCIDENTS,... I THINK THE OWL IS READY FOR RELEASE.

as they must have the calcium in their diet needed for growing strong bones. Stirring in some powdered bone or other source of calcium (ask a chemist) and a vitamin additive will do the trick – keep the hair of the dog to enable some form of pellet to be coughed up.

When you release your short-term invalid, choose a spot close to where you found it and release it at dusk. There should be enough light for you to see how the bird goes: can it fly really well, was it struggling, did it come down awkwardly? It is obviously rather irresponsible to try to release a bird if the weather is really rough – either wind or rain. Remember that you have little chance of a second go if the bird has recovered and it is a good idea to have two or three people present in case it has to be taken back into captivity for further treatment. Testing the bird in a large room is always a good idea but make sure that the windows are masked so that it does not brain itself, and think how you are going to recapture it should it prove to be really fit (carefully, with a net, for instance). If the bird cannot be caught at all try opening the window for it to return to the wild.

If you are able to weigh your casualty this will give a good idea as to whether it is in poor condition. Unfortunately the weights of the two sexes of the five usual species of owls found in Britain are quite different – particularly during the breeding season. A big female Tawny, at any time of the year, will often weigh more than 600g (21oz) but few males reach 500g (18oz). The list below tells you when to worry about a weight of a British species. A live bird, otherwise looking fit, at or below these weights may have something further wrong with it or, at the very least, should be fed up a bit before release.

Species	Worrying Weight
Barn Owl	270g (9½oz)
Little Owl	140g (5oz)
Tawny Owl	350g (12½oz)
Long-eared Owl	220g (8oz)
Short-eared Owl	260g (9oz)

For definite females (ones you know have laid eggs, or have well developed brood patches) add 10%.

Orphans?

Young owls, all cuddly and covered in down, are rescued by well meaning people everywhere every year. Although they look pathetic, they are seldom really orphans and the worst thing anyone can do, in most circumstances, is to rescue them by taking them home and feeding them on bread and milk (yes, really) or even a proper carnivore's diet.

In general these are young birds that have started to explore the area round their nest and they are still being looked after by their attentive parents. By all means rescue them from the middle of the road or the clutches of your dog or cat but, if at all possible, leave them in the same area to fend for themselves – with their parents' help. The most humane way of dealing with them is to lob them into the branches of a nearby tree – so that they do not become a fox's snack – and leave them to it. These apparently helpless youngsters are very adept at climbing, using their strong claws and beak, and may even make it back up the rough bark of an oak or similar tree to the nest-hole six or seven metres above the ground. Their calls will tell the parent birds where to deliver the next meal.

Orphans? No. Suitable cases for treatment? No. All they possibly need is a helping hand and to be left alone.

Breeding for release

Most thinking people nowadays realize that keeping a bird cooped up in a cage, for their own personal enjoyment, is a selfish indulgence which deprives the bird of its right to a free wild existence. Strangely, the records clearly show that birds kept in captivity almost always outlive their wild cousins by many years – but what dull and boring years. Many people are even becoming worried about keeping owls in zoos, though their presence increases awareness of their interest and beauty – a necessary prerequisite for a good public image and therefore proper protection and conservation. It is *not* the intention of this book to give advice on long-term owl keeping, which is really a task for the expert.

The reader with an interest in keeping owls will immediately ask, how, if you are not going to tell me, do I learn to become an expert? The only answer is by becoming a real nuisance to those who have already learnt from others or through experience what to do. There is one circumstance where a potentially valuable contribution to the welfare of owlkind is being performed by keeping birds in captivity. That is by breeding healthy young birds from disabled parents, for release into the wild in areas where the wild population has disappeared.

It is good to know that a couple of road casualties, with broken or amputated wings and so no chance of release, are being kept in right royal conditions and are producing young birds for release. Unfortunately there are cons to put against the obvious pros. For instance there may be a good reason why there are no wild owls in a particular district; releasing captive-bred birds to die a lingering death, through lack of food, is clearly not a very good idea. Similarly the unthinking release of birds into an area where the natural, wild population is as dense as the food supply will sustain is disruptive.

This being said, the efforts of several groups, who are particularly concentrating on Barn Owls, may represent the species's best chance of re-occupying many of the areas from which it has disappeared over the last couple of decades. Indeed it might well be argued that the release of such captive-bred young, even before the area is ready for them, can be justified especially if food supplements are given to the released birds. Such releases are almost invariably done in an unoccupied and newly nest-boxed site so the birds are not simply cast into unknown territory. The birds for release start off with a period in a spacious cage, or enclosed in a large barn, which

remains the home base for supplementary feeding.

Although Barn Owls are the species most often reared, Tawny chicks can also be raised quite easily. However Tawny parents in the wild put a lot more effort into rearing the young after they have left the nest than Barn Owls do, so supplementary feeding at the time of release, and for a long time after, is essential. Barn Owls can produce many more young, in a captive situation, than Tawnies since the pair may start breeding in February and carry on well into the autumn. The eggs of one pair, if incubated artificially and hand-raised, can produce a couple of dozen chicks in a single year. These youngsters are likely to become imprinted on humans and not realize that they are owls. Such a situation is very sad and totally negates the point of trying to release birds into the wild. Not only will the owls be very unlikely to breed, but they may fly up to people and try to perch on shoulders or heads – most disconcerting and likely to get a bad press for owls in general.

So much internecine strife (see p. 89) takes place in some areas that there are also serious worries that the release of some species of owl may have a bad effect on other species in the vicinity. This may not be an important factor in Britain but in areas of Europe, where Eagle Owls have become scarce or extinct, the other species of owls are doing very well; they could be decimated if the Eagle Owls were to be reintroduced. The results of reintroductions and the increasingly effective protection of Eagle Owls are now causing problems in many parts of northern Europe. The news that a feral pair of Eagle Owls raised a youngster in Scotland in 1986 was very exciting but may not bode too well for other Scottish owls.

Owls and gamekeepers

A few decades ago any bird or beast that showed any inclination to kill and eat other birds or beasts was immediately branded as an enemy and pursued, to the death, by all gamekeepers. That is probably a simplification of what went on but it is undoubtedly true that they were looked upon as direct competitors for the available game. Whereas British owls rarely, if at all, take game birds, the presence of large numbers of naive game bird chicks in a rearing pen might be too much of a temptation. Sometimes when the rearing pens are in a lazy Tawny Owl's territory the owl may do a great deal of

damage. Unfortunately no proof of damage used to be needed – its talons and hooked beak were enough to prove the owl's guilt.

The introduced foreigner, the Little Owl, was particularly maligned – without any proof of damage. Indeed careful investigations of food from Little Owl pellets and also from stomach contents have proved the bird innocent in almost all circumstances. Still the persecution continued with gun and trap. For many keepers the easiest way of dealing with the owls was to erect a pole overlooking the rearing pen and to put a trap on it. This caught any bird that perched on it in a totally indiscriminate manner. Blackbirds and Song Thrushes were just as likely to be caught and die a horrible death as the hawks and owls for which it was intended.

Happily this is now illegal; many, probably most, keepers would never dream of using such a trap even in the secret recesses of their own woods. Clearly, since their living depends on the presentation of a good number of Pheasants for the guns in the autumn, they will still kill rogue Tawny Owls attracted time and again to the easy meals. However most keepers now take care to proof the pens against the attacks of the owls rather than try to kill the owls themselves. Anyway, over the last 50 or 60 years, the gamekeeper has become more of an endangered species than the owls as the large estates have broken up and their staffing has been streamlined.

Protective acts

In Britain all owls are now protected under the Wildlife and Countryside Act. This means that they may not be killed or caught in the wild except under licence. For killing such licences would only be given for very good reason and are very rare; catching licences are given for scientific investigations – for instance to ringers who want to mark birds. Protection for all species was first introduced in 1954 with the Wildbird's Protection Act.

The rarest species, the Snowy Owl, is specially protected during the breeding season – because of the unique breeding pair on Fetlar, Shetland, for several years. The Barn Owl is also on this list (Schedule 1 under the Act) since its populations have declined so badly over the last few decades. It is illegal to approach an occupied nest of either of these species or to inspect it, without having previously obtained a special licence from the Nature Conservancy Council. It is *not* illegal to go about your lawful business, for

Signs on the tree: "PLES CNOK IF AN RNSR IS REQUID", "HAVE VALID NCC. LISENCE REDDY", "WOL'S HOUSE", "GAMEKEEPRS ONLY PLEZ RING FOR RESPONSE"

(AFTER E.H. SHEPARD)

instance in farm buildings where there is a Barn Owl nest, as long as you do not wilfully disturb the birds and interfere with their breeding cycle.

Over most of Europe owl species are also protected – rather recently in some instances. However shooting of some species to protect game still goes on, particularly in rural areas. In parts of Italy Little Owls are still taken into captivity to be used as lures to trap small birds as they mob a captive owl (see opposite).

In Britain it is perfectly legal for anyone to have in their possession an injured owl that they are treating, without a licence, but it must be passed on to a Licensed Rehabilitation Keeper within a short while. These are often local enthusiasts and many look after all bird casualties from a wide area – often calling themselves Bird Hospitals. Such keepers are registered with the Department of the Environment, Tollgate House, Bristol; and the individual birds will be marked and registered if they have to be kept in captivity as they cannot be released. All healthy owls in captivity have also to be so registered and will have either a closed ring placed on their leg at a few days of age (if born in captivity) or a special tie mark.

It is not illegal to have moulted feathers from owls in your possession but any body (including stuffed owls) or eggs should only be in your possession if you can show that they were not originally taken illegally. Thus a Barn Owl found dead on the road can be picked up and you can even pay the local taxidermist to have it mounted for you. Any sale or transfer of ownership of eggs, bodies, stuffed owls or live owls needs to be subject to a licence from the DOE. Live birds are often transferred, whether fully fit or crippled, from person to person to try to breed them in captivity. This is quite easy with some species like Barn Owl and extensive programmes of reintroduction are taking place to make up for losses over the last thirty years.

These reintroductions are controversial, since many are taking place without proper planning and follow-up. What happens is that people with crippled owls find they are able to breed lots of young birds from them and simply release them into the wild in 'suitable' sites where a nest-box is provided. Often the suitability of the site rests on evidence (even hearsay) that Barn Owls used to be in the area years and even decades earlier. Since they may have gone because the ecology of the area has changed and is now no longer suitable for Barn Owls such reintroductions may be rather unfortunate as the newly released bird will either have to move away or rely permanently on food supplements.

Owl scandal

In northern Italy even today many hundreds, possibly as many as five thousand, Little Owls are taken into captivity each year by small-bird hunters. They are treated pretty well for they are essential decoys for the autumn's and winter's sport. The Little Owl is fitted with a harness and perched in a suitable spot for songbirds to be attracted to mob it. In some areas the songbirds used to be caught for cageing but most often they are shot simply for sport.

The capture and cageing of the Little Owls, in the first place; the small-bird hunting itself, and the use of the live Little Owls as decoys should all be illegal under the European Community's Bird Directive. However, the complicated legal situation in Italy and EEC exemptions have, as yet, not enabled the bird protection lobby in Italy, led by LIPU (the Italian equivalent of the RSPB) to outlaw this particularly unpleasant activity.

Folklore

Owls have certainly not been ignored: references to them abound in the myth and legend of all sorts of cultures within Europe and worldwide. Interestingly, there is no clear consensus as to whether they are, in general, a 'good thing' or a 'bad thing'. As might be expected, because of the weird sounds they make in the darkness of the night they have a fairly bad reputation in many areas; equally, on the basis of sympathetic magic, there are almost as many stories putting them with the good guys.

Owls have a lot going for them in both respects. Their eerie calls ranging from almost human screams, sudden frightening hunting calls to rhythmic hoots and snores, could be given almost any interpretation – and they have been. They call at night when the senses are sharpened and most of the rest of nature is quiet. If one is normally tucked up asleep one does not realize just how much noise they make or how many call to each other over long distances. Add to this an upright stance, big and bright eyes and a large head with an almost human face and small wonder that stories abound.

Legends about the wisdom of the owl can be traced back several thousand years to the time when the owl was the symbol of the Greek Goddess of wisdom, Pallas Athene; it may even go back further to the association of an owl with one of the primitive gods that preceded the Greek pantheon.

> A wise old owl sat in an oak,
> The more he saw the less he spoke,
> The less he spoke the more he heard,
> Why can't we all be like that wise old bird?

The associations with death, bad news, childbirth, war, etc., seem mostly to be negative; they probably result from people hearing the unaccustomed night-time noises of owls when having to stay awake on a death-bed vigil, sentry duty, etc. There is even a widespread association between thunder and owls. Certainly there are many records of thunder provoking owls to call and a sudden clap of thunder will wake both the owl and the human observer.

Of course the omens provided by owls were as nothing to the incredible recipes which were produced to utilize the whole or part of the owl. The witches in *Macbeth* simply wanted a young owl's ('howlet's') wing for their cauldron, but particular bits of owl were important for specific uses. Powdered burnt feet of an owl, taken internally, were a specific against snake bite. The heart and right foot of an owl placed on a sleeping person would act as a truth drug. Various bits of owl applied as ointment to the eyes would give excellent night vision. Owl's eggs eaten before the event were also thought to be an excellent aversion therapy to the excesses of alcohol!

HEALTH WARNING:
OWLS USED AS LIGHTNING
CONDUCTORS CAN BECOME
DANGEROUS

Whole owl was also 'heap big medicine' in many areas: the birds were nailed up over the entrances of houses or barns to avert the 'evil eye'. The association with thunder also, unfortunately, gave rise to the use of a dead owl, again nailed up on the portal, as a primitive – and pretty ineffective – lightning conductor. In parts of China the four corners of the roof had representations of owls to ward off lightning. It is quite possible that the openings deliberately left for Barn Owls in the hay-lofts of many farm buildings in northern Britain and southern Scotland may have a hint of this protection against lightning – as well as a more plausible wish that the birds would pick off some of the local vermin! These cultural manifestations of owls go right back into pre-history. One of a famous series of cave paintings in France clearly depicts a nest with adult and young Snowy Owls. This is in an area now far to the south of the Snowy Owl's range but then, of course, the ice was still retreating northwards.

Shakespeare showed keen observation of animal behaviour and when referring to

> . . . The owls by day,
> If he arise, is mocked and wondered at.

in *Henry VI*, he must have been referring to mobbing.

However he also used the owl as a bird of ill omen, just as it was considered in classical times, in *Julius Caesar*:

> Yesterday the bird of night did sit,
> Even at noonday, upon the market-place,
> Hooting and shrieking,

An author who obviously had a liking for owls was Sir Walter Scott. Of several happy references to owlkind the following must be one of the most gracious:

> Of all the birds in bush or tree
> Commend me to the owl;
> For he may best ensample be
> To those the cup that troul.
> For when the sun has left the west,
> He chooses the tree that he loves best,
> And he whoops out his song, and he laughs out his jest
> Then, though hours be late and weather foul,
> We'll drink to the health of the bonny, bonny owl.

Scientific names explained

For many groups of birds the scientific names, awarded them by taxonomists over the years since Linnaeus first formulated the rules, provide an interesting commentary on the evolution of ideas of relationships between birds. Obscure little warblers and various similar species of all sorts of birds have, as their specific names, a wide variety of tags indicating the problems faced in determining their relationships. *Dubius, difficilis, neglecta, inexpectata* are all names indicating difficulty in telling the species apart.

Others are descriptive: *flavi-, rufi-, cyano-, acro-* mean 'yellow', 'red', 'blue' and 'arrow-shaped' respectively, and *-cephalus, -collis, -gularis, -rostris* mean 'headed', 'necked', 'throated' and 'billed'. Hence *flavirostris* is the scientific, specific name for more than a dozen birds of all sorts.

Many other forms of descriptive name are used. *Elegans, major, minor* and *madagascariensis* are pretty obvious. Sometimes the names of people, often well-known ornithologists, are Latinized and made into the official scientific notation. This has happened with explorers, too, as we owe America to Amerigo Vespucci. Examples in the bird-world with half a dozen or more species to their name are Hartlaub, Hodgson, Newton, Sclater, Taczanowski and Temminck.

Not much recent imagination has been needed in naming owls in Britain and Europe: many of them were known to the Greeks and Romans and thus have perfectly good Greek or Latin names which could be 'borrowed' by the taxonomists. The following seem to be the derivations for our birds:

Tyto alba   Barn Owl
Tuto is Greek for a kind of owl – possibly derived from the hooting. *Alba* is white.

Strix aluco   Tawny Owl
Strix is Latin for screech-owl (Tawny) and may be derived from the Greek word meaning to screech. The *aluco* is from the Greek.

Otus scops   Scops Owl
Otus is Greek for an owl with long ears and *skopos* is the actual Greek name for this species.

Asio otus   Long-eared Owl
Asio is Latin for this species.

Asio flammeus   Short-eared Owl
Flammeus means 'flame coloured': not very descriptive of the bird's plumage or even eye colour, and possibly coming from the amazing colour it can take on if seen over marshland by the light of the rising or setting sun.

Athene noctua   Little Owl
Athene is after the Greek Goddess and *noctua* is Latin for some kind of owl (we don't know which) – it incorporates the root *nox*, meaning night.

Aegolius funereus   Tengmalm's Owl
Aigolios is a Greek name for a specific kind of owl (unlikely to have been this one) and *funereus* means ill-boding or funereal.

Country names

As highly conspicuous birds, owls have attracted to themselves a huge number of country names throughout Britain. These have been recorded in a variety of books through the years but one of the best and most recent is *All the Birds of the Air* by Francesca Greenoak – she documents more than there is space for here.

Many of the names are similar for the two widespread species (Barn and Tawny) and it is clear that there was not necessarily proper distinction made between the two; 'Madge Howlet' was used in some areas for one and in others for the other, and the Welsh *Aderyn corph* or *Aderyn-y-cyrph* – the corpse bird – can be applied to both. Perhaps the Gaelic names are better – *Cailleach-oidhche Gheal* ('white old woman of the night') and simply *Cailleach-oidhche* ('old woman of the night') for Barn and Tawny respectively.

For the Barn Owl many country names are descriptive ('White Owl' or 'Hoolet', 'Hissing Owl', etc.) and others have obviously derived from the general 'owl' root: Woolert, Owlerd, Ullat and Hullart. But for many others there seems to be no obvious explanation: Billy Wix (or Billy Wise), Jenny Owl, Padge or Pudge, Gil or Gili Owl, etc. The birds are often found in churches and so Church Owl is no surprise. The Barn Owl has 34 different names and variations listed by Francesca – the other four British owls rate only 56 between the four species.

Most refer to the Tawny with descriptive ones to the fore – Brown, Golden, Grey, Hollering, Screech, Wood and Ivy feature. There are still Billy Hooter, Gilly Hooter, Jenny Hoolet and Jinny Yewlet to match the folksy names given to Barns. Long-eared gets 'horny' names like Horn Coot, Hornie Hoolet and Tufted Owl. In the Shetlands it is also called Cat Owl but this is also used of Eagle and Snowy Owls (particularly Catogle). Short-eared names refer to its mousy tastes on moorland – Mouse Owl, Moss Owl, (many moorland areas in northern Britain are called mosses), Moor Owl, Marsh Owl, etc. Its migrations to and from Britain, over the North Sea, give rise to Woodcock Owl (they arrive at the same time), Pilot Owl and Sea Owl. In Shetland they are variously called Brown or Grey Yogle.

The Little Owl is a newcomer introduced to Britain only a relatively short time ago. It is not surprising that there are no local folksy names but quite a few 'coined' ones indicating knowledge that it came from abroad: 'Belgian', 'Dutch', 'French', 'Spanish', 'Little Dutch' and even 'Indian'. One of the introducers, Lord Lilford, is remembered around his home area in Northampton by the owl named after him – Lilford Owl!

Little angels

In some parts of the country the night-time calling of the owls was linked with the angels. Thus the Barn Owls became known as Cherubims and the Tawny Owls as Seraphims. This may have arisen because so many churches used to have Barn Owls living in their towers. Certainly in several parts of the country generations of small children were raised believing that the phrase:

*   'To Thee Cherubim and Seraphim continually do cry' was all about the white owl screeching and the brown owls hooting through the night.*

To owl

Owls, being creatures of the night, have given their name to a variety of other creatures: there is the 'Fern Owl' in Britain – a country name for the Nightjar; there are 'Owl Parrots', 'Owl Monkeys' and 'Owl Moths' in various parts of the world. 'Owl-light' is an alternative name for the uncertain period between night and day – the gloaming.

One of the strangest uses of their name is in the verb 'to owl', or commit 'owlery'. This was a specialized form of smuggling practised when much of Britain's wealth was based on sheep and their fleeces. The trade with France, particularly the woollen mills of Flanders, was strictly regulated, with levies being charged on exports of wool (or sheep) across the water. As always where artificial embargoes are put on trade and where there is a profit to be made, a thriving illegal business grew up. This became known as 'owlery' and so 'to owl' was to smuggle sheep or wool from Britain to France.

It is tempting to suggest that the name may have been derived from the Norse word for wool – 'oo' or 'oue', still in use in Shetland – but the smuggling was mainly a *southern British occupation. The use of the word owl was surely simply an association of the night bird with the nocturnal activities of the free-traders.*

Wise old owl

There can be little doubt that a good number of owls are pretty old – certainly when compared with the life spans of smaller birds – but are they wise? Wisdom is not really the sort of attribute that one ascribes to an animal but, in its own way, the old territorial owl is very wise indeed.

The only way that a bird is able to survive is by being well adapted to its surroundings. It must know where its next meal is coming from, how to shelter from the wind, the rain, the cold and the snow and, most important, how to avoid those accidents which tend to shorten the lives of all wild creatures. For the owls these include unwelcome encounters with larger owl species, speeding cars, thin and invisible wires and so on. To be able to cope, the owl must learn from its experience – that this perch is likely to provide a

WISE?..... OR HOT ON FACIAL EXPRESSIONS?

succulent rustle if you are patient for long enough, this hole is warm and sheltered for a nest, a roost in the depths of this ivy-covered tree trunk is not likely to be disturbed – even that a spot of hunting on this railway embankment is safe until the 7.19 from Paddington comes along.

If learning from experience can be called wisdom there seems little doubt that old owls are wise.

Owl doom?

The many stories of owls predicting death and doom have very deep and long-standing roots. They may be traced back through many different cultures and clearly have come about spontaneously in many different areas. It is not difficult to see why, as owls are strange night-time creatures and often have harrowing and piercing calls. Small wonder that such superstitions have built up over the centuries. However there may be a grain of truth in what has become associated with the birds. As many of the temperate species of owl are relatively early breeding birds, their main time of territorial dispute, and therefore calling, tends to be in late autumn and winter.

This is just the time when the weather begins to become cold and, in earlier days, life began to get harder. There were therefore likely to be rather more human deaths than at other times of the year. Also most households kept to daylight hours and tended not to use too much in the way of artificial light as it was expensive. When someone was mortally ill there would surely be someone keeping vigil as the mortal body yielded up its immortal soul. During the long lonely hours the watcher is sure to have heard calling owls which would have been unremarked by those normally sound asleep. Thus the calls of the owls would tend to be associated with death.

Studying owls

Owl study can become a real obsession, with one's year punctuated by the different aspects of owl behaviour: winter and early spring to map the territories, spring to record the nesting attempts, summer to follow the fate of the youngsters and, all the year through, pellets to find and analyse.

Obviously a great deal of interest and enjoyment can be had from putting together various of the activities mapped out in this book – making, erecting and checking nest-boxes, analysing pellets, checking territories, etc. – but to some people this may not be enough. Some specialist activities can be self-taught, with the aid of handbooks, such as nest-recording, but others, like ringing or radio-tracking, require 'hands on' training.

Nest-recording is one of those activities that several hundred members of the British Trust for Ornithology undertake every year. Very simply, the fullest possible details that can be obtained, without putting the nest at risk from disturbance, are gathered for each nesting attempt and are recorded on a standard card. This is then returned to the BTO HQ in Tring where the information, with that from other nest-recorders throughout the country, makes a valuable record of the whole breeding season throughout the UK for the owls concerned. The number of cards received is never enough and the more that are sent in, the more accurate the information can be. First of all one starts to build up a general picture of what happens, then regional and annual differences become apparent and, finally, analysis can begin to unravel all sorts of information on the pressures on the populations of owls, and how they cope. Full details of the Nest Record Scheme and sample cards and instructions can be obtained from the BTO (see over).

The National Bird Ringing scheme is also run by the BTO (I am in charge of it). All our ringers have to be properly trained before they are able to go off by themselves. It is possible to train as a general ringer in a couple of years with a good, active trainer. People solely interested in owls may be able to qualify, just for owl ringing, rather quicker, and certainly without having to handle several thousand birds of a variety of species.

The rings used on owls, as for other species, are metal and include a return address as well as a unique serial number which identifies the bird as an individual. Specialist ringers of other species sometimes use coloured rings to enable the birds to be identified in the field – not much good with an owl in the dark. Indeed it is very difficult to go out deliberately to catch fully grown owls and the vast majority, of all species, have been ringed as nestlings. The best bet, for trapping adults, is to lure them into nets using tape-recordings of their calls (see page 97). There are fairly strict guidelines as to what can be done because too persistent a use of tapes could disrupt the local bird's idea of who was where.

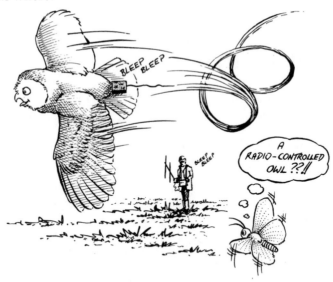

One high-tech means of following the birds is by radio-tracking. This also needs special training – and a good deal of money and time. Generally the radio-packs, which are now very small, are fitted by a ringer to the bird either by gluing them to tail feathers or by affixing a neat little rucksack-like back harness. These enable the person with the right sort of directional receiver to follow the marked birds throughout the night and find out what they are doing and where they are doing it. The results show the size and shape of the home range and the use made of different perches within it. For many birds solar-powered packs are used – but obviously these don't work for owls, so radios tend to pack up after a week or two when the battery runs out.

NUMBER OF OWLS RINGED AND RECOVERED IN
BRITAIN AND IRELAND

Species	Ringed	Recovered
Tawny Owl	13,058	1,010
Barn Owl	7,293	1,199
Little Owl	5,223	352
Long-eared Owl	2,247	166
Short-eared Owl	1,398	93
Snowy Owl	27	4
Scops Owl	3	0
Tengmalm's Owl	2	0

Figures correct to end of 1985.

Further reading

There are many books with passing references to owls and hundreds, even thousands, of scientific papers describing their anatomy, taxonomy, behaviour, food, movements, breeding strategy, etc. Anyone seriously interested in owls in Britain and Europe should start off by consulting the books listed below:

Handbook of the Birds of Europe, the Middle East and North Africa (volume III), editor-in-chief Stanley Cramp (Oxford University Press, Oxford, 1983)
This is the compendium of facts and figures with enormous detail and a very good list of references. Known by most birders as 'BWP' – after its sub-title *The Birds of the Western Palearctic.*

Owls of Europe, Heimo Mikkola (T. & A. D. Poyser, Stoke-on-Trent, 1983)
This is particularly good on the ecological relationships within owls and between the owls and their prey.

The Barn Owl, D. S. Bunn, A. B. Warburton & R. D. S. Wilson (T. & A. D. Poyser, Stoke-on-Trent, 1982)
Written by three bird-watchers obsessed with the Barn Owls of their own

areas, this has a wealth of personal observation spanning years of study.

Eric Hosking's Owls, Eric Hosking with Dr Jim Flegg (Mermaid, London, 1982)
Stunning photographs of owls worldwide taken by the master of bird photography.

Owls of the World, editor John A. Burton (Peter Lowe, London: revised edition 1984)
Fourteen authors contributed to this overview of owls which provides a good introduction to those from outside Europe.

In addition specialized information on distribution in Britain should be investigated first through the two atlases produced by the British Trust for Ornithology and published by T. & A. D. Poyser – *Breeding* (Tim Sharrock) and *Winter* (Peter Lack). They have entries for each species for each 10km square in Britain and Ireland. More detailed information is available through the increasing number of local atlas maps being published which, generally, deal with squares of 2km sides.

General information on the care of all species of sick and injured birds and other animals can be found in *We Save Wildlife* by Les Stocker (Whittet Books, London, 1986). Some useful information is contained in other books like *First Aid and Care of Wild Birds,* edited by J. E. Cooper and J. T. Eley (David and Charles, Newton Abbot, 1979). However, I would urge anyone wanting to take this up firstly to think twice about the dedication and time needed to do it properly – and not doing it properly is worse than not doing it at all – and secondly to go and pester someone who is doing it successfully so that they do not make all the old mistakes again.

Organizations
There is no British Owl Friends Fellowship or other organization dealing only with owls. However there are two national general bird organizations that owlers should be interested in joining. BTO (British Trust for Ornithology), Beech Grove, Tring, Herts HP23 5NR, deals with national investigations like nest recording, common bird census, atlas and ringing. It also has a system of regional representatives and links with local bird societies – many too numerous to list here. The RSPB (Royal Society for the Protection of Birds), The Lodge, Sandy, Beds SG19 2DL, is the organization concerned with setting up reserves, protecting rarities – and much more. Their wardens looked after the Snowy Owls of Fetlar – one of their Scottish reserves. And the Mammal Society is concerned with their diet (see p. 47).

Index

The main characters, the five British owls (Barn, Little, Long-eared, Short-eared and Tawny) appear so often that their entries are not included.

Accidents, 102, 104, 105
African Marsh Owl, 12
Age, 102, 104
Aggression, 68, 77, 90, 98
Atlas, 91, 92, 127

Barred Owl, 45
Breeding, 17, 20, 68-70, 76, 82, 84, 85, 91-5, 98, 110, 111, 115
Brood patch, 73, 74
BTO, 65, 91, 92, 95, 124, 125, 127
Burrowing Owl, 12, 20

Calls, 9, 11, 21-31, 36, 37, 80, 92, 94, 96, 116, 121, 123, 124
Camouflage, 8, 25, 71, 88
Captive breeding, 98, 110, 111
Captive owls, 99, 102, 110, 111, 115
Census, 85, 92, 124
Clutch, 9, 71, 75, 76
Collision, 102, 104
Copulation, 69
Country names, 17, 120, 121
Courtship, 68

Decoy, 115
Disease, 102-104
Display, 27, 55, 69, 70
DOE, 114, 115
Drowning, 106

Eagle Owl, 10, 11, 25, 26, 52, 53, 60, 71, 72, 76, 79, 90, 91, 98, 111, 112, 120
Ears, 8, 9, 32-5, 42
Eggs, 9, 36, 56, 69-76, 108, 111, 117
Elf Owl, 13
Evolution, 8, 9, 14, 15, 60
Experiments, 33, 34

Eyes, 8, 30, 33, 37-41

Facial disc, 9, 12, 21, 26, 28, 30, 33
Feathers, 8, 15, 33, 42, 103
Feet, 33, 43, 44
Fishing, 12, 42, 50
Fishing line, 105, 106
Fledging, 79, 80, 89, 109
Flight, 17, 42
Food, 9, 37, 45-54, 68, 75-82, 88, 89, 109

Game rearing, 105, 112, 113
Great Grey Owl, 30, 35, 58, 59, 72, 76, 79

Hatching, 74, 78
Hawk Owl, 12, 13, 26, 27, 30, 58, 59, 72, 76, 79, 82
Head, 37, 38
Hunting, 22, 24, 28, 30, 32, 34, 37, 39, 75, 88, 90

Imprinting, 111
Incubation, 68, 71, 72, 74, 76
Inflatable owls, 99
Injury, 107
IWC, 91

Latin names, 11, 118-20
LIPU, 115
London Wildlife Trust, 86

Mapping, 95-7, 124
Migration, 11, 80-84, 91-4

NCC, 65, 113
Nesting, 12, 13, 17, 18, 20, 28, 36, 37, 55-67, 71, 73, 74, 77, 79, 91, 109, 110, 115, 124
Nictating membrane, 41
Nomads, 84, 85, 90, 91

Omens, 116, 118, 123

Pair-bond, 68, 69
Parental guidance, 104
Pellets, 9, 45-52, 67, 88, 113

Pesticides, 72, 73
Plumage, 42
Populations, 124
Powerful Owl, 12
Prey, 9-30, 34-6, 42-7, 49, 51, 54, 65, 70, 74, 75, 85, 90, 104, 106
Pygmy Owl, 10, 27, 28, 41, 58, 59, 71, 72, 76, 79, 90

Radio-tracking, 125, 126
Railway, 104, 106
Reintroduction, 110, 111
Roads, 50, 102, 104, 106
Roost, 21, 24, 86-8, 94, 99, 123
RSPB, 115, 127
RSPCA, 107

Scops Owl, 11, 24, 25, 31, 32, 53, 59, 72, 76, 79, 81, 90, 94, 119
Sex, 55, 68, 69
Shooting, 105, 106
Snowy Owl, 11, 17, 18, 23, 58, 59, 68, 72, 74, 76, 79, 88, 90, 91, 94, 102, 113, 117, 120, 126
Studying owls, 94, 97, 115, 124, 125
Stuffed owls, 99

Tape recording, 65, 97, 125
Tengmalm's Owl, 11, 30, 31, 41, 58, 59, 72, 76, 79, 82, 90, 94, 120, 126
Territory, 9, 20, 24, 26, 36, 61, 68, 80, 82, 85, 88, 89, 92, 94-9, 112, 122, 124

Ural Owl, 28, 29, 30, 40, 59, 60, 65, 72, 76, 79, 90

Weight, 10, 11, 18-29, 108
Wildlife & Countryside Act, 17, 65, 113
Wildlife Hospitals Trust, 127
Wing, 10, 11, 15, 17, 20-29, 42, 72
Wisdom, 116, 122, 123